A Quantum of Gestalt

A Quantum of Gestalt:

Physics, Spirituality and Gestalt therapy

Brian O'Neill

Developed and Published by the Ravenwood Press a subsidiary of Illawarra Gestalt. P.O. Box 141 Peregian Beach, Queensland AUSTRALIA.

Cover illustration, text design and art work: B O'Neill

ISBN - 1480215554

For more information on Ravenwood Press Email: boneill@uow.edu.au Website: www.illawarragestalt.org

Or write to

Brian O'Neill Illawarra Gestalt Centre P.O. Box 141 Peregian Beach, Queensland Australia

Contents

Spirituality, Poetry and   13
Physics in Gestalt Therapy

Relativistic Quantum Field Theory   37
and Gestalt Therapy - An Overview

Field Theory in Psychology   67
and Gestalt therapy

Quantum Field and   83
Gestalt therapy - A Lived Wisdom

Commentary to Relativistic   91
Quantum Field Theory -
Implications for Gestalt Therapy

Initial Clinical Applications of   101
Quantum Field Theory within
Gestalt Therapy

Field Theory of the Couple: 115
Poetry, Spirituality and Physics Meet

Gestalt Family Therapy -   141
A Field Perspective

David Bohm: A Quantum   175
Physicist providing Insights to
Psychotherapy and Spirituality

Addendum: 195
Understanding Field Theory in Physics

Bibliography   227

Dedication

As with Sir Isaac Newton
in my writing on physics I have stood on
the shoulders of giants.

I dedicate this book to the work of
Albert Einstein
David Bohm and B J Hiley
for their gift of an
Undivided Universe.

Acknowledgement

To my dear friend
Malcolm Parlett
For his continuing support
in all matters of the field.

Spirituality, Poetry and Physics in Gestalt therapy

Arjuna:
What are Nature and Self?
What are the field and its Knower,
knowledge and the object of knowledge?
Teach me about them Krishna.

Krishna:
I am the Knower of the field
in everybody Arjuna.
genuine knowledge means knowing
both the field and the Knower

The Bhagavad Gita

The Rare Reader

I hope the title of this chapter offers a challenge, even an excitement in the bringing together of such seemingly divergent terms as "spirituality", "physics" and "poetry". In my work in various settings I find a growing number of gestalt therapists are interested and curious about such connections emerging.

When I started university in the early 1970s I was studying to be a physicist before switching to psychology (with a double major in English Literature). I remember I was excited at the time to read a book by Le Shan (1974) entitled "The Medium, Mystic and Physicist". His argument, put simply, was mediums, mystics and physicists described the world in a similar fashion. However this was not obvious and it was the rare reader who would indeed see these convergences. I was one of these rare readers.

This 'rare' reading continued as I went from studying physics to English Literature and psychology. I also became interested in and explored spiritual texts and finding connection between these wider fields of study. Writers from physics, literature and psychology said similar things using different words. My comparison uncovered further common ideas - a rewarding and mind broadening awareness in which today I still find joy and richness.

A useful place to begin exploring the connection between spirituality, physics and the poetry of Gestalt therapy is the origin of the term "field". The origin of the term in the English language, including the sources it arises from, provides common meaning in some instances between these seemingly different areas of study. Some definitions fit with Gestalt therapy and provide links with Hindu philosophy, physics, poetry and the work of Martin Buber (which is poetic in itself).

Physics Poetry and Gestalt Therapy

The Shorter Oxford English Dictionary on Historical Principles (1978) offers three groupings of definitions for the word "field" showing how it arose historically into the English language from various sources, which in summary are –

i.   From the Old English "feld" which is Ground and compared to town or village. (1697)
ii. An extended surface or large stretch; an expanse (1577)
iii. derived from Middle English as an area or sphere of action (such as a battle 1678). Also in Physics (1863) it is the area or space under the

influence or within the range of an agent.

The historical derivative of the word field can be developed further in the use of the term 'organism/environment field' (Perls, Hefferline and Goodman). The word 'environment' (1603) first described to set a limit or *boundary* (environs) and 'organism' (1604) defines an:

- organic structure;
- *organized system or whole* of dependant and independent parts and
- organized body.

These historical derivatives combine to paraphrase 'organism/environment field' as

the experience of a boundary of an organized system or whole within a sphere of action which is under the influence of an agent.

17

It is worth noting the 'self 'is defined in Perls, Hefferline and Goodman as the 'agent of growth'.

Gestalt, Physics and the *Bhagavad Gita*

My interest in the historical roots of words and their meaning was stimulated years later when I read the word "field" within an ancient Hindu classic, the *Bhagavad Gita*. This text is described as the decisive moment in the history of India and Indian spirituality in 300-200 BC (Griffith, 1983).

The *Bhagavad Gita* is part of an epic poem, the *Mahabharata*, and viewed by many as the supreme in Hindu teaching and one of the greatest religious documents of the world (Prabhavananda and Isherwood (1944, edition 1987). The poem begins with discussion between the warrior Arjuna, a king, and Krishna, who personifies God. At chapter thirteen I was surprised and fascinated to read the chapter title *"The Field and Its Knower"* as this fitted with modern gestalt ideas about the self and the field perspective.

From the beginning of this chapter in the *Bhagavad Gita* this use of the term 'field' stands out and we read –

Arjuna: "I wish to learn about Prakriti and Brahman, the Field and the Knower"

To understand these terms of Field (Prakriti) and the Knower of the Field (Brahman) it helps to know Hinduism, where the same words are used at different levels with different meaning. The reader must understand the context of the level to know which meaning of the word is being used.

To answer Arjuna Krishna says clearly –

"The body is called the Field because a man sows seeds of action in it and

reaps their fruits. Wise men say that the Knower of the Field is he who watches what takes place within the body."

In the literal sense Khrishna describes to Arjuna similar ideas of reality to those of Merleau-Ponty describing life as 'lived-through-world'. In both the body plays a vital part in self identity. This fulfils Husserl's idea of giving flesh to an idea by realizing it in concrete terms. As we read in Perls, Hefferline and Goodman:

"And in breathing one sees par excellence that the animal is a field, the environment is 'inside' or essentially pervading at every moment. And so anxiety, the disturbance of breathing, accompanies any disturbance of the self-function; thus the first step in therapy is contacting the breathing."

Perls, Hefferline and Goodman,

1952, pg 401)

This first definition of 'field' in the *Bhagavad Gita* harmonises with Gestalt therapy defining the person, and the *'physiologically phenomenal field'* perspective.

Next in the poem Khrishna takes a leap across levels of meaning and having defined the personal he jumps to Brahman, the Absolute –

"Recognise me as the Knower of the Field
    in everybody"

This leap of Krishna fits the transcendental field of Merleau-Ponty; the transcendental phenomenology of Husserl; and the transcendental philosophy of Kant. Each of these authors uses the original meaning of terms to mean *transcendent*. Hindu philosophy in defining reality this way offers a bridge between the knowable and the unknowable. At this level of meaning 'Brahman' (The Knower) is now no longer man as he is described within Western philosophical approaches to knowledge. He is now 'Brahman' and 'Prakriti' (or Maya) which is all mind and matter – the 'Field' in a wider sense, similar to physics. The Bhagavad Gita in a few lines moves from personal awareness of self and the body to an awareness of the 'All'. Krishna is the Knower of all - from the personal self to the Godhead.

Faraday in the 19th century offers a similar shift in levels of context in physics as Krishna in the *Bhagavad Gita.* He makes a bold leap of imagination in a lecture in 1844 on the nature of atoms. As with the leap in context Khrishna offers to Arjuna, Faraday turned the nature of reality from the personal to the universal. He proposed that rather than seeing atoms as physical objects which give of a web of force, *the web of force itself is the reality* and the atom existed as a concentration in that web.

He used a thought experiment to describe this.

He asked the audience to imagine the Sun sitting in space by itself. What would happen if the Earth suddenly appeared in its place? How would the Sun know it was there? Before the Earth appeared the web of forces associated with the Sun – the field – spreads throughout space. As soon as the Earth appeared it would impact on this field of force. This impact would tell the Earth the Sun existed. In this way the 'Field' is the reality the Earth experiences, not the Sun itself.

Faraday argued these lines (or webs of force) filled the universe and is the reality by which these seemingly separate entities are connected - a field perspective. The material world of atoms and suns are like "knots" in the various fields of force. In Hinduism, individuals are like "knots" of being in the reality of Brahman - in which Krishna is the Knower of this field.

Perls, Hefferline and Goodman offer a similar description of self and field not as an analogy or metaphor but as reality.

> *"In a certain sense, the self is nothing but a function of the physiology; but in another sense it is not part of the organism at all, but is a function of the field, it is the way the field includes the organism"*
>
> (Perls, Hefferline and Goodman 1951 pg 400-401)

This description of the self in Gestalt therapy fits with the 'Imagination Experiment' of Faraday in 1844 and agrees with the same description of self in *The Field and the Knower* in the *Bhagavad Gita* over 2000 years ago. A rare read indeed.

Einstein affirms this view of reality when he combines matter and energy though he found it difficult to take the final step unifying field and 'matter/energy' are one. He states he could not imagine it in his usual way using his 'Imagination Experiments' (Isaacson, 2007). Other quantum physicists such as Bohr and Bohm included awareness as an essential part of reality and defined awareness with an equation for all their calculations. David Bohm extended these earlier concepts in physics by offering a holographic description of reality where each part contained the whole.

Physics, Spirituality and Dialogical Therapy: The Poetry of Martin Buber.

Buber and Dialogue are key pillars in gestalt therapy and with Buber much of what he writes translates to quantum physics. Comparing his writing with what

Faraday talked about 'knots of energy', Buber states it this way –

> "*The world of 'It' is set in the context of space and time. The world of 'Thou' is not set in either of these... there exists the unbroken world of 'Thou': the isolated moments of relations are bound up in a life of world solidarity*"
>
> (Buber,1958, pg 8)

So the world of 'It' is atoms and suns, which seem separate, and the field world of 'Thou' is quantum reality. This quantum reality is the web of force (Faraday) connecting everything and is essentially real.

Or to quote Buber further –

> "*The human being is not a He or She, bounded from every other He or She, a specific point in space and time within the net of the world; nor is he a nature able to be experienced and described, a*

26

loose bundle of named qualities. But
with no neighbour and whole in himself,
he is Thou and fills the universe."

(Buber, 1958, pg 8)

Early in my study in psychology I discovered Steven Rose, a neurophysiologist, who in his book *The Conscious Brain* talks of the many levels in understanding the brain –

- quantum structure of atoms;
- molecular properties of the chemicals which compose it;
- the electron-micrographic appearance of the individual cells;
- the behavior of the neurons;
- the evolutionary or development history of these neurons;
- the behavioral response of the individual;
- familial context and social environment of the person.

In comparing the holistic and reductionist perspectives of reality, he uses *'being in love'* as an example:

"Each of these descriptions may be complete in its own terms, yet which one is relevant must depend on the circumstance. A statement about a particular human being, 'He is in love', could b provided with a description at any one of these varying levels. It could be in terms of the social interactions of the particular human; of an analysis of his own 'state of mind'; of a specification of the changes in hormonal level in his circulating blood stream and variations in sensory input; the altered firing patterns of the cells of the hypothalamus and cortex; new synapses in particular brain regions; changes in the rates of synthesis of proteins or other macro-molecules; changes in the quantum state of atoms composing his body".

(Rose, S., 1976)

I read Rose many years ago while completing my psychology degree and still find his example of these levels of description useful to determine the frame of reference in operation when discussing a phenomenon. Every experience has a physical, emotional, psychological, social, and spiritual aspect. Deciding which of these labels to attach to the experience depends on our perspective, context, background, and belief system.

The *Bhagavad Gita* uses a word such as 'field' within a context that is either the personal or transcendent. It operates as both. Rather than lessen its meaning in relation to other contexts as if they are exclusionary, it uses a particular level of meaning where each connects and support the other in a 'both/and' framework, rather than 'either/or'.

These different levels defining a phenomenon are only a problem when it is argued 'as if' only one level is correct. This is what that Latner (2008) calls the "Reality Fight". To not reduce all meaning to one level and instead explore and learn from this stairway of meaning has the opposite effect to the reality fight. There is an expansion of meaning and not a lessening.

Being open to physics, poetry and spirituality as aspects of the organism/environment field and Gestalt therapy finds harmony with the founders of gestalt therapy who embrace a "unitary approach" (Perls, Hefferline and Goodman 1951, pg 228). This encourages appreciation of each area of study and level of meaning.

Field Theory in Physics and Gestalt Therapy

At present physics accepts the idea of 'field' as a reality, while many Gestalt therapy writers relate to 'field' epistemologically (as a metaphor or method). Parlett (2005) hinted at the exciting implications for Gestalt therapy in re-visiting the science which provided the conceptualisation of field theory to consider current relativistic quantum field theory. Physics began with the simple concepts of mass, force, vectors and inertia which described the mechanics of the world and universe. In this classical Newtonian physics, there are separate objects and separate forces which act on these objects. Similarly the history of psychology began with theories of inner and external forces which acted on or in the individual through psychological drives, reinforcement, will and motivation and unconscious processes. This is the consensus reality of the western World. It is how we construct our state of consciousness and our experience of separate identity (Ornstein 1972, Tart 1975).

In physics a new idea appeared - the field. At first with electromagnetism and then light, this idea proved experimentally successful in describing and predicting reality. At first the field represents vectors of force in a schematic drawing of forces (such as gravity) and is therefore a representation of reality, not reality.

Field as Representation

This first stage developing a field perspective of reality was through visualising and mapping the vectors of force acting in a field. At this point the field was simply a device to help with conceptualization. By drawing lines of force such as gravity, physicists noted the direction of the force, but they could not use this to explain gravity. So describing the field as *more* than a representation (or model) seemed fruitless (Einstein and Infield 1938). The field remained a tool - a field *theory* or method.

Field as Real

Newton's laws had defined the motion of the earth as affected by the force of a sun far away (the so called 'action at a distance'). It was the work with electricity, magnetism and electromagnetism which saw the field become a reality. Maxwell described both electric and optical phenomena and the new idea of the field as *here and now,* as a whole, not two separated events. As Einstein and Infield (1938) state this was the most important discovery in physics since Newton. With the arrival of Maxwell's four equations describing the structure of the electromagnetic field, there was born, in Einstein's words, "a new reality".

"The electromagnetic field is, for the modern physicist, as real as the chair on which he sits"

(Einstein and Infield, 1938, pg 151)

The field had changed from being an epistemology (a method) to an ontology (description of reality) - no longer field theory but *the field* as real.

Field and Matter as Real - the Relativistic Quantum Field

Einstein hoped this would lead to a Unified Field theory, where matter was points of concentrated energy in the unified field. He combined energy and matter and now wanted to explain matter as a concentrated form of field, the 'knots in the web of force'.

He said it became impossible to imagine a surface separating mass and field, try though he might. This, and the arrival of experiments that needed an acceptance of discontinuous quanta of energy and matter, left Einstein with the conclusion that he had two realities – matter and field.

"The theory of relativity stresses the importance of the field concept in physics. But we have not yet succeeded in formulating a pure field physics. For the present we must still assume the existence of both: field and matter."

(Einstein and Infield, 1938 pg 245)

The existence of these two realities, field and matter, as described by relativity and quantum physics together, led to the name of Relativistic Quantum Field theory (Bohm 1993). Separately neither relativity theory nor quantum theory fully explains the phenomenon of light but together they do as relativistic quantum field theory.

Bohm (1993) plays a central role in developing a syntheses of both relativity and quantum physics. This was at first a hybrid called Relativistic Quantum field theory, and later the theoretical development of the holomovement (based of holographic reality). This is what Bohm terms the 'Implicate Order' as he wrote in his final text with Hiley *The Undivided Universe.* In the next chapter we will explore relativistic quantum physics and how it parallels Gestalt therapy in describing a field perspective.

Relativistic Quantum Field Theory and Gestalt Therapy - An Overview

Quantum theory and quantum mechanics developed through understanding experiments and observations which show the *appearance* of the dual nature of reality. Light is a prime example. There are times light behaves *as if* it were composed of particles or photons (such as with the photoelectric effect) and other times it behaves as a wave phenomenon (such as bending light around an object). Interestingly there are times light behaves as both a wave and a particle. Further the nature of light as particle or wave is *dependent on whether it is observed or not.* This is known as the "wave-particle duality" (Einstein and Infield 1938, Bohm and Hiley 1993, Lightman 2000).

The quantum view of reality offered four points which challenge relativity and the classical view of reality. These are the wave-particle duality; the uncertainty of measurement; the nature of the observer in determining reality; and non-locality or entanglement. These four ideas of quantum physics can be defined psychologically as Identity, Connection, Ontology and Control, as described in the table below -

Physics	Psychology
Wave Particle Duality	Identity - awareness of separate self yet also self in relation to others
Non locality or entanglement	Connection - how our relationships define us
Reality and the inseparable nature of the observer and the observer	Ontology of Self - Experience of separate self and 'self in relationship' paradox
Uncertainty	Control - free will and determinism

In comparing relativistic quantum field theory with Gestalt therapy four areas link each and describe a bridge between them -

38

1. Quantum Identity and the Wave Particle Duality.

In the famous Double Slit Experiment originated by Thomas Young, a dim light passes through two slits in a board and projects unto a screen which produces a pattern. This pattern displays light acting as a wave phenomenon. The pattern shows positive and negative interference in the forms of striated bands. If the light was acting as a particle they would instead produce two clearly defined bands of light.

When the light is watched by non-interfering glass monitors attached to the slits each electron or photon is now recorded as they pass through. In this case the photon or electron acts as a particle (as matter) instead of a wave phenomenon.

When the photon or electron is observed it acts as a particle, yet when not observed the result is a wave phenomenon. (Lightman, 2000) This is called the wave-particle duality where identity is both matter and field. Perls, Hefferline and Goodman (1951), describe this dual nature of self as the 'system of contacts" and "agent of growth' duality. This was not clearly articulated in Perls, Hefferline and Goodman (Crocker, 1999) and thus Gestalt theory describes a similar duality of self as relativistic quantum theory.

We are a particle (agent of growth) and a wave phenomenon (system of contacts in the organism/environment field). Perls, Hefferline and Goodman's original idea of self correlates with that of physics - we are field and matter, aware of our unique nature and at the same time intrinsically part of an organism/environment field. We are in the field and of the field. We are the Field and the Knower as described by the *Bhagavad Gita.*

Perls, Hefferline and Goodman highlight the 'field' nature of the self. Authors such as Fritz Perls (as shown in his Gestalt prayer) focused later on the individualistic, particle nature of self - "You are you, and I am I" (Shepherd, 1976, pg 3). Kempler (1974) stated the Gestalt movement (at his time) was out of balance giving too much emphasis to 'I am I' with not enough appreciation of union. The theme of separateness and union is developed by both Wheeler (1991) and Polsters (1973).

> *"Contact is not just togetherness or joining. It can only happen between separate beings always requiring independence and always risking capture in the union. At the moment of union, one's fullest sense of his person is swept along into a new creation. I am no longer only me, but me and thee make we."*

Gestalt Therapy Integrated

Polster and Polster, page 99

41

2. Quantum Connection and the phenomenon of Non Locality

The 'EPR' experiment, named after Einstein, Podolsky and Rosen is the most emphatic description of a quantum experiment which challenges both classical physics and relativity. This famous experiment describes two seemingly separate halves of a molecule spinning in opposite directions large distances apart with an instant connection between them. It was designed to critique quantum mechanics but had the opposite effect. As one half is measured this causes a shift in the other immediately. Such a result displays "action at a distance" which shows a wave phenomenon. This happens at a speed which is instantaneous and violates the universal constant of light. Bohm (1993) explains it as a field phenomenon where the active information in the field connects each to the other, similar to the Faraday experiment.

"It is as if the two particles were in instantaneous two-way communication exchanging active information that enables each particle to 'know' what has happened to the other and to respond accordingly"

(Bohm, 1993, pp 203)

The connection between seemingly separate particles can be an explanation for psychic and mystical phenomenon. This describes the field more as a 'whole' experience and less a 'separate self' experience. Several authors refer to this as the spiritual nature of relativistic quantum field theory (Le Shan 1974), (Capra, 1982), (Talbot, 1991) and (Wilber, 1985).

The dual nature of our identity described by the EPR experiment is at the heart of the writing by Martin Buber about I-Thou. It provides a lens to understand his deeply mystical and personal style of writing. This work is the ground for dialogical psychotherapy, which has a strong influence in Gestalt therapy. As Buber writes -

> " The human being is not a He or She, bounded from every other He or She, a specific point in space and time within the net of the world; nor is he a nature able to be experienced and described, a loose bundle of named qualities. But with no neighbour and whole in himself, he is Thou and fills the universe."

(Buber, 1958, pg 8)

Describing the separate person as 'whole in himself' (particle nature) Buber paradoxically states he is a 'Thou' which fills the universe (field or wave nature). The person is a "both/and", matter AND field, whole in themselves AND filling the universe.

In Gestalt therapy this provides a frame to explain the experience of "I-Thou". Using physics terms the experience of "I-Thou" is the separate individual awareness becoming aware of their field nature rather that their particle nature, or as Hycner states,

"By the very recognition that there is something larger present in the therapy situation than just the sum of the total of the individuals physically there, this is already a recognition of the 'more than personal'"

(Hycner, pg 97).

Hycner describes the Hasidism story of the holy sparks in a fashion similar to the halves of the molecule in the EPR experiment. The holy sparks are separated yet mystically connected and contained in all things as the source of wholeness. In the Hasidism story meeting as people (containing the holy sparks), is like the separate molecule halves being nonetheless connected. It is this connection we experience as the "between" of dialogical therapy.

3. Ontology and the Phenomenological role of the Observer

Bohr believed the indivisibility of the wave and particle nature of a quantum of energy meant the entire phenomenon was a single un-analysable whole. It is this whole that makes up the entire quantum phenomenon (Bohr, 1961 in Bohm 1993). He argued we cannot discuss the properties of a particular system apart from the context of the entire experimental arrangement including the observer and the measuring apparatus with which these properties are observed.

The fundamentally new aspect of quantum theory is the whole is more than the sum of the parts. This offers significant support for the Gestalt therapy perspective of the human personality.

Van Neuman (Bohm 1993) developed the concept of the "many worlds" theory to explain this wholeness of the quantum phenomenon as well as the separateness of classical Newtonian physics. He stated that before a phenomenon was measured it existed in many different potentials, or worlds, and the process of measurement, observation or awareness created one of these worlds.

Others physicists found "many worlds" untenable. Instead they have described this process in phenomenological terms as the "many minds" theory. Therefore each different possible measure of the phenomenon was a certain perspective of mind and there are an infinite number of phenomenological realities possible at the quantum level (Bohm 1993). This is similar to the idea in Gestalt therapy of co-created realities between people where our experience, while being unique to us, has many potential realities and when shared with others becomes new and co-created.

The Mouse that Observed

Awareness plays a key part in quantum physics and there are mathematical equations to define awareness as part of the whole quantum potential. Since Heisenberg and Bohr, observation was interactively part of the whole. It is interesting for a Gestalt therapist to read physics texts with awareness in the index; find equations for the awareness of an observer; and see physicists tackle defining awareness as part of the quantum whole. Von Neuman proposed that observation (or awareness) induces a collapse of the wave function into a single state (that is into an observed reality where before there was a range of possibilities). Einstein objected saying he could not believe a mouse could bring about a drastic change in the universe simply by looking at it. Everett argued that it was the system was affected by an observation but the observer becomes 'correlated' to the system. The mouse does not affect the universe – only the mouse is affected. (Bohm, 1993)

As the mouse IS a part of the universe, the universe is also affected. When two people look at each other they each affect the other. A physicist might say they 'correlate' to the other. Our phenomenological field is a 'special case' of the wider quantum field potential that exists. Awareness by and of itself has an effect and as we become aware of each other we change each other. This supports the current work on relational fields (Yontef, 1993). It links to the co-existence of phenomenological (perceived) and ontological (real) dimensions of the field as described by Crocker (1993).

4. The Uncertainty of Quantum Control - Individuals and Crowds

Einstein pointed out the laws of quantum physics are statistical as they cannot measure or control an individual system (Uncertainty Principle). They look instead to a series of repeated measurements. This led him to state -

"Quantum physics deals only with aggregations, and its laws are for crowds and not for individuals"

(Einstein and Infield 1938 p286)

Bohr and Heisenberg were the main authors of the Uncertainty Principle which, unlike the previous views of reality, did not allow for individual measurements and predictions but only probability estimates of aggregates. This has meant physicists letting go of the predictive control of classical Newtonian physics, adopting the statistical estimates of quantum physics.

Gestalt therapy does not try to measure or "control" the individual as a separate person (like most psychology) but studies the operation of the contact boundary in the organism/environment field. Gestalt therapy works with wholes in line with Bohr in physics.

Earlier theorists talked about Gestalt therapy and the need for the therapist to exercise control of the therapeutic situation, defined as "the therapist being able to persuade or coerce the patient into following the procedures he has set" (Fagan and Shepherd, 1970, pg 91-92). This was clearly a movement away from the principles tenets which are now in the fore front once again.

Current theorists such as Hycner (1993) describe a paradoxical process of the searching for balance between choice and acceptance. This is described in the original text of Perls, Hefferline and Goodman as the "middle mode" of being. This is in between directive and passive functioning, where the person is accepting, attending and growing into the solution. It is characterised by the substitution of readiness (or faith) for the security of apparent control. (Perls, Hefferline and Goodman, 1951; 1984 edition). In this way Gestalt mirrors quantum physics, 'letting go of predictive control' in being attuned to what is existent.

Field theory in Psychology and Gestalt therapy

While physics in a body reinvented itself from the frame of reality of Newtonian physics to that of relativistic quantum field theory, psychology witnessed a partial expression of this with the work of James, Smuts, Lewin, and Gestalt psychology. Most psychology however remained in the reductionist world of Descartes, and Newton, where separate individuals can be measured, experimented on and predicted.

Psychologists who adopted a field theory understanding (like Lewin) did so at the level of field as a representation or epistemology. Others (like modern day physicists) adopted a new view of reality. In this view the field is not described as a theory (or epistemology) but as reality. Gestalt therapy has both of these ideas of field theory. At times Gestalt therapy is in line with modern physics, where observations affect the nature and identity of the observed. The 'connectedness' of the organism/environment field and the relativistic quantum field of physics are clearly more in tune than reductionist models of human behavior. These offer simplistic cause and effect results in therapy, similar to classical Newtonian physics. Newtonian physics is a limited special case of quantum reality similar to 'cause and affect' psychology which could be defined in the same way.

In the following section, early theorists who described field theory in psychology are considered, and how they have shaped Gestalt therapy's development.

William James

James, as the father of American psychology, was clever in his time to have considered the field as an idea relevant to psychology. He used the term to understand the structure of consciousness and formulated the idea there were "fields of consciousness" rather than the traditional reductionist units of thought or memory or an idea. He states -

"...it (field of consciousness) is nevertheless there, and helps both to guide our behavior and determine the next movement of our attention. It lies around us like the 'magnetic field', inside of which our centre of energy turns like a compass needle, as the present phase of consciousness alters into its successor."

(James 1902 in 1977 edition p. 233)

James offers a unique beginning in this area of psychology and the field perspective. It is the beginning of an idea that the classical Newtonian reality of separate parts was limited in our understanding of reality in psychology.

Gestalt Psychology

Gestalt psychology is a field theory psychology with a strong influence on Fritz and Laura Perls. It was with the work of people such as Wertheimer, Koffka, Kohler,

Fuchs, Gelb and others we find their ideas carried over into Gestalt therapy. This includes the work of later authors, in particular that of Kurt Goldstein in neurophysiology and Kurt Lewin in social science (Ellis 1938, Bowman 2005). Gestalt psychology focused on perception and related areas such as animal experiments, thought, psychic forces, and pathological phenomena (Ellis 1938). The original work by Wertheimer shows the relation to the later work of Perls, Hefferline and Goodman. The basic formula for Gestalt theory, as outlined by Wertheimer (1938) describes the field similar to Gestalt therapy-

> *"There are wholes, the behavior of which is not determined by that of their individual elements, but where the part-processes are themselves determined by the intrinsic nature of the whole"*
>
> *(Wertheimer, 1925 in Ellis 1938, pg 2)*

Wertheimer was clear that Gestalt psychology was not a separate entity in itself but a convergence of scientific and philosophical standpoints. It was as functional as mathematics, in which a formula, whether mathematical or psychological, had a dynamic functional relationship to the whole. This included Gestalt psychology's view of the ego, seen as a part of the total field, with the whole process operating in the field affecting behavior. The interconnectedness of identity within a field perspective is clearly obvious.

The connection to the later theory of Gestalt therapy is also clear. The organism is part of a larger field of organism and environment, and the behavioral concepts of stimulus-sensation are replaced by changes in field conditions and the total reaction of the organism (Wertheimer, 1925). Wertheimer in a statement predating the concept of self in Gestalt therapy goes further to talk of the meaningful, functioning whole of a group of people, such as children or South Sea Islanders. In such situations the "I" rarely stands out alone and it is the wider organism of the group which exists. Finally, he challenges mathematics need not only deal with piecemeal situations but with the mathematics of the whole, and in a predictive way suggests that quantum physics may force mathematicians to consider 'mathematics of the whole situation'. It could be argued that Wertheimer was right. It is also worth remembering that these early Gestalt psychologists were two decades before Gestalt therapy.

Kurt Lewin

Lewin (1951) described Field theory as an epistemology (or methodology) in that it is simply a way of understanding reality and not the reality itself. He equates it to a handicraft, in that methods like field theory can only be understood learned and mastered by continuing practice.

> *"Field theory is probably best characterized as a method; namely, a method of analysing causal relations and building scientific constructs". (Lewin, 1951, pg 45)*

Behind the field theory of Lewin appears a wish to express human behavior in scientific, mathematical terms. Borrowing from physics, he talks of psychological force, power fields and the direction and velocity of behavior and notes the parallel between time-space quanta and his own idea of "time-field-units" (Lewin, 1951)

> *"I am convinced that these concepts which we use for the representation of psychological facts, like region, spacial*

relationship in life force, connectedness and separateness, belonging, etc., are real spacial concepts in a strict mathematical sense. It is very important for psychology to use these concepts in a strict and consistent way"

(Lewin, 1936, pg 42)

Lewin discussed the strict and consistent use of these psychological ideas in mathematics, equivalent to the mathematics of physics. However he intentionally avoided the use of models from physics as, while of value, models involve serious dangers. They contain much that is purely arbitrary and this goes against the strict definitions needed. So it makes sense that Lewin views field theory as a method and not a model. This reluctance to use models from physics is perhaps one reason there is a virtual absence of physics in his work. Lewin makes passing reference to electromagnetic and gravitational fields, though at one point mentions having discussed his work with a leading theoretical physicist. He notes physics and philosophy have not developed field theory to be helpful to psychology, while psychologists interested in field theory have not been successful in making it clear.

"The only excuse I know of is the matter is not very simple". (Lewin, 1951, pg 43)

It is more in mathematical modeling that Lewin is inspired and field theory is a vehicle (or in his word, method) to hold his quasi-scientific methodology of the mathematics of behavior. A flaw in his approach is the lack of quantification in numbers of the mathematical terms and formulae he uses.

He draws these life spaces and field forces in a similar way to which physicists draw vectors of force. This is clearly not the organism/environment field theory of Perls,

Hefferline and Goodman (Perls, Hefferline and Goodman), though it may have influenced it. There is no mathematics of behavior, or topological drawings in Perls, Hefferline and Goodman and no suggestion that Gestalt therapy is purely scientific method.

Jan Smuts

Smuts (1926) provides significantly more detail than Lewin in outlining the scientific ground he uses to build his theory. He describes electromagnetic and biological fields and connects his work with relativity and the beginnings of quantum physics. There is no emphasis on the mathematics needed to do this and instead Smuts uses a language of connection and holism which is strikingly similar to Perls, Hefferline and Goodman. Smuts pays significant attention to physics and to the work of Einstein. He believes that while the work of physicists are "a terror to the uninitiated", it can be simply and intelligently discussed by distinguishing between the viewpoint and the difficult mathematical processes (Smuts,1926, pg 26). This pre-dates the work Einstein did ten years later to make his theories clearer for all without mathematical formulae. (Einstein & Infield, 1936). Smuts places "field" within the history of science and brings an epistemological cohesiveness and integration to physics, biological and psychological field theory. In doing so Smuts displays a scholarly understanding of the field theory of physics and psychological field theory. The organism and the field as described by Smuts are more akin to the writing of Perls, Hefferline and Goodman than that of Lewin, as he speaks of "the system of organic regulation"; "co-ordination amongst an indefinitely large number of parts"; "self restoration" and the "system of co-operation amongst all its parts which makes them function for the whole" (Smuts, 1926, pg 65). In his moving beyond mathematics to wholeness, and the term coined by Smuts, "Holism", we see a clearer influence on the field theory of Perls, Hefferline and Goodman - an influence imbedded in physics and biology. The prime work of Smuts is in bringing physics theory to a level of understanding the field of Life and Mind and not only Matter. In writing akin to the Wave-Particle duality of physics, Smuts writes -

"A natural whole has its "field" and the concept of fields will be found most important in this connection also"

(Smuts, 1926 pg 96).

This is strikingly similar to the current view of the wave-particle duality in quantum physics which views the matter-field phenomenon as a particle (natural whole) accompanied by its wave function (i.e. field).

As Bohm states -

"...electrons enter the system one by one. Each one will have its own quantum field..."

(Bohm, 1993, pg 410)

It is with this conceptualization of Holism that Smuts offers the possibility for a bridge joining the work of quantum theory and Gestalt therapy, before Gestalt therapy was developed. He states -

"The Field is the source of the grand Ecology of the universe. It is the environment, the Society - vital, friendly, educative, creative - of all wholes and all souls. It is not a mere figure of speech or figment of the imagination, but a reality..."

(Smuts, 1926, pg 369)

Field Theory in Psychology and Gestalt Therapy

There are many influences on Gestalt therapy and the theoretical and philosophical ground is indeed rich. Few would disagree that field theory is a core philosophical underpinning, and yet the construct of field theory has not seemingly been well understood, discussed or applied to practice.

In Gestalt therapy there is no clear sign whether field theory is mainly a theory and method of understanding reality (ie epistemology) or a description of that which exists and is real (ie is ontological) or an integration of both.

From the various influences which have shaped its development Gestalt therapy carries both possibilities, that field theory is an epistemological method and an ontological reality. Few gestalt therapists have dared to venture further to relativistic quantum field theory or the holographic field of Bohm (1993) or Sheldrake's (2003) morphogenic fields. Parlett calls for further extension of our thinking in his current writing on field theory -

"No discussion of the field in the specialized and relatively small scale arena of Gestalt therapy should ignore the general scientific beliefs of the day. (Parlett 2005 p.61) "

He goes on to state it would be ironic if Gestalt therapists were to turn their back on these scientific developments which might well confirm the emphasis in Gestalt therapy of field theory. Perls, Hefferline and Goodman (1951) offer an ontological description of the field as a whole - an organism/environment field. In essence this is not a field *theory*, more simply there is the field.

This is similar to Smuts, where the field explains the nature of the ontological reality of wholes and holism. If we take Perls, Hefferline and Goodman as the starting point of literature in Gestalt therapy, Gestalt therapy is "field" from the outset. While "field theory" is not listed in the index or the content page, the book is awash with the conceptualisation of the

"organism/environment" field, proposed as a reality (ontology) and not only a theory or model (epistemology). It may be fair to argue Perls, Hefferline and Goodman is less field theoretical and more field ontological - in short a description of the field, as it exists - "... the original, undistorted, natural approach to life"

(Perls, Hefferline and Goodman, 1984 edition, pg viii)

Yontef (1993) argued that by the 1980's there was no clear description of field theory and that people would espouse being field theoretical and then talk more about dialogue and phenomenology and say little if anything about field theory itself.

"Frankly I think I am clearer when I discuss phenomenology or Gestalt psychology, even about aspects of field theory, than when I discuss field theory directly. So, out of a good sense of tactics, cowardice, laziness or ignorance, I often teach phenomenology and dialogue and less often directly discuss field theory"

(Yontef, 1993, p.292)

Joel Latner (1983) and Malcolm Parlett (1993, 1997) as well as Yontef, have reversed this trend of sparse writing on field theory and Parlett (1993) in particular is an advocate for the work of Kurt Lewin. Later works by authors such as McKewen (1997), Zinker (1994), Wheeler(1991), Resnick (1995), Crocker (1999), Staemmler (2006) and Gaffney and O'Neill (2008) have brought field theory more into the foreground of the literature. In the conceptualization, training and practice of Gestalt therapy, field theory is by many accounts the most challenging area of our theoretical ground. As Yontef states:

"Talking and reading about field theory and understanding it is very difficult, perhaps the most difficult aspect of Gestalt therapy theory to discuss"

(Yontef, 1993,p.286)

Yontef also cautions against the use of the term to confer status and prestige, sometimes as if it were a religious icon - "invoked to get a positive and revered response" (Yontef, 1993,p. 292) As Robine

71

(2001) points out there are also a variety of ways in which people have used the term field theory as a concept including the organism/environment field of Perls, Hefferline and Goodman; those meaning the background or environmental context; the Lewian field of forces; and a phenomenological field. Robine also mentions Sheldrake's morphogenic field and how a field can create form. Similarly Francis (2005) lists some current uses of the term field in the British Gestalt Journal - the field of experience; the field of the soul; the erotic field; the phenomenological field and the pre-phenomenological field. He also mentions the work of Sheldrake and Bohm.

The Field - Model, method, metaphor or reality?

Theoreticians at times are at the edge of wondering is this simply a theory they are describing or something more. Malcolm

Parlett draws close to this edge when he states –

"One of the confusions that arises for newcomers to field theory relates to what 'the field' actually is. Is it simply a metaphor or analogy, or this there an imputation of some actual 'energy field'. In the author's view the status of the concept is generally metaphorical. "

(Parlett, 1997, pp 19)

He immediately begins the next sentence with "However..." and goes on to list revolutionary and awesome developments in modern physics and other sciences which show the field may be real. As we have seen in physics, the nature of reality is a core issue and unfortunately there is not one clear theoretical definition. At present there is matter and field. There exists a tension between relativity and quantum physics, around the phenomenon of non-locality,

73

and this has been instrumental in physicists to developing theories which house both, such as Bohm's holomovement and the Implicate Order (Bohm 1993).

Does the same tension exist in Gestalt therapy and is it timely to begin discussing theories which synthesize various theories of the field? Can we learn from these developments and synthesis in physics? And will this be useful to our theory and practice as Gestalt therapists? At first Lewin viewed field theory as method and no more, yet Smuts clearly saw this as a way of defining reality. These two influences on Gestalt therapy may been seen in our literature where for example Perls, Hefferline and Goodman is principally an ontological definition of an existing organism/environment field, while the work of those such as Yontef tends more to the Lewinian concept of an epistemological tool, as does Parlett. Yet it is Parlett who also offers a challenge to the purely epistemological nature of field theory and urges us on to consider the implications of the advances in physics and biology. So the answer to our first question is, yes, there is a divergent view of field theory in Gestalt therapy literature. These differences can perhaps be understood in several ways. Yontef (1993) in his response to Latner's (1983) work on linking quantum physics to Gestalt therapy, defines three types of field theories in Gestalt therapy -

- Linear, which is seen to be a mechanistic form of field theory using Newtonian language;
- Non-linear, is more "right brain" universal language field theory, with a spiritual flavour;
- and the Integrated approach, found in Gestalt psychology which allows for differentiation and wholes

Latner was critiqued by Yontef for using a typology of Newtonian and post Newtonian field theory, and also in this earlier article used a typology of field theory linked to the Gestalt therapy institutes and their various approaches. Yontef was critical of this and stated he preferred a typology based on "conceptualisations and not geography", not the use of ad hominem arguments, and to put aside what he saw in Latner's writings to be a typology of sectional and personal rivalries (Yontef, pg 384). Paradoxically if this sectional rivalry exists, such rivalry will influence and colour the field perspective and this influence can be an important discussion in and of itself.

The development of definitions of field theory through following and listing the conceptualisations of the various writers, can be classified using the typology in the following table -

Gestalt therapy writing about field theory	Basic elements and/ levels of understanding field theory
No mention of field theory	No attention to field theory and these include the later work by Perls himself.
A **Knowledge** of field theory	Describe field theory; reference other authors and their definitions of field theory. Field theory is usually a short section without any detailed analysis of critical appraisal. It is taken as a "given".
Understanding of field theory in a singular sense. The "either/or" approach	Describe field theory and critical analysis More advanced work in this area may compare and contrast models, but eventually settles for one model above others and in a way "chooses" the "right" field theory.

Gestalt therapy writing about field theory	Basic elements and/ levels of understanding field theory
An understanding of the **Paradoxical nature** *of field theory.*	*Few writers and their hallmark is to accept more than one field theory at the same time, even though they may develop different conclusions or perspectives.*
The "both/and" approach.	*This includes, for example, accepting phenomenological and ontological fields together; or linear, non-linear and integrative field theories; or seeing the epistemological and ontological properties of field and field theory. This has been developed in the use of the term the "field perspective"*

It would seem possible to "place" various authors and books in the sections of these tables and classify them accordingly, or even more fittingly ask them (those who are still alive) to do this themselves. As a method of classification it helps note the depth and understanding writers have of the field perspective.

The difficulty and error in doing this would be to accept there exist discrete quanta of conceptualisation, and this could be a more sophisticated way of assigning a "geography" of field theory critiqued by Yontef, with "place" now resting in these boxes on a table.

In essence, this typology is more a description of levels of explanation available to all writers and students of field theory - they are more like steps on a stair way, as opposed to discrete cells. Each author will be able to move up and down these levels of conceptualisation, and some tend however to remain mainly on one favourite step of understanding of the field perspective.

This typology is derived from the Swedish theologian Swedenborg, who stated simply -

> "People have knowledge, intelligence and wisdom. Knowledge has to do with being acquainted with something, intelligence has to do with understanding it, and wisdom has to do with living it".
>
> (Swedenborg,1768,
> edition 1992 page 137)

These first steps on the "stairway" are principally about knowledge and understanding of field theory, yet the direct lived wisdom of the field is an altogether different matter and will not reduce to books or articles. The degree and use of the conceptualizations gives a clue to the a field theory author's connection with a 'lived reality'. The lived reality of field in Gestalt therapy, like quantum physics and spirituality, is marked by paradoxical conceptualisations found in the fourth category, which is clearly "both/and" thinking rather than "either/or".

This last area of the lived wisdom of field theory can of course exist without a detailed conceptualization, yet like the pieces of a hologram, this will be a diluted figure compared to the whole. The more we integrate theory skill and practice in our work as therapists and in training, the more we can hope for field knowledge, field intelligence and field wisdom.

Quantum Field and Gestalt Therapy - A Lived Wisdom

Yontef (1993) in his earlier essays on Gestalt therapy field theory and physics, treats these advances in physics in the same way as does Wilber (1985) with spirituality - they both offer a strong word of caution to not simply adapt these exciting developments without first chewing them over. They both remind readers in their respective areas of study that physics is neither Gestalt therapy nor spirituality and there are distinct differences between the subject matter of each. They also warn against a populace acceptance of physics as having prestige and social power as a way to promote various authors ideas of field theory. These cautions are clearly worth noting, and that being said, the earlier writing of each of these authors rests on literature in physics which is not as current as the work of physicists such as Bohm and

Hiley (1993) or with the more integrative work of Sheldrake (2003) in biology. In this chapter we will consider implications of these advanced ideas in physics for the theory and practice of Gestalt therapy.

1. Convergence of models

The first use for Gestalt therapy of relativistic quantum field theory is the support it gives to the holistic and "esoteric" world view of the gestalt therapist, among so many other "research driven" or "scientific" modalities. While gestalt therapy has not traditionally paid particular attention to scientific confirmation, it is comforting to realize the principles of Gestalt therapy are supported by the relativistic quantum views of reality.

Gestalt therapists have been espousing a reality of dialogue, phenomenology and field which are well supported by current world views of physics. In many ways the traditional scientific approaches of Cognitive Behaviour Therapy and others are operating within a classical Newtonian framework which is at best a special and limiting case of the wider reality as described by relativistic quantum field theory. Like quantum physics, Gestalt therapy now calls for a new way of research and consideration of outcome studies.

2. The Mathematics of Consciousness

Quantum mechanics has shifted from a world where the physicist could justifiably stand outside of that which was being measured, to a world where the measurement and act of measuring decides the nature of that which is being measured. So the observer has become part of the mathematical equation and this has lead to the mathematics of awareness wherein the awareness of one observer (person or computer) is defined as an equation. These mathematical equations are more valid examples of reality and the field than the quasi mathematical modeling done by Lewin. Currently this is the application of mathematics by physicists to define and include awareness as part of quantum theory and to the inclusion of consciousness as a quantum phenomenon. Bohm (1993) in presents consciousness as an unfolding and enfolding between the classical world and the quantum world - a bridge between both realities which is in part a particle (or matter) phenomenon and in part a quantum field effect. Consciousness is a wave-particle duality.

In a description approximating that of Perls, Hefferline and Goodman, Bohm (1993) defines classical reality as *being a special case of quantum reality*. Such a process involves collapsing a wave phenomenon mathematically. This leads to describing the classical physical world as a special limited case of quantum reality and the concept of independent existence is an illusion, as stated in Perls, Hefferline and Goodman. Yet as Bohm points out the illusion rests in seeing the classical world as the whole. Once it is seen to be merely a facet of the whole, and not the whole, it is no longer an illusion. This supports Crocker's (1999) discussion of phenomenological and ontological fields and challenges the therapist to hold both co-created realities and the possibility of that which is AT THE SAME TIME is real and standing out - what Van Dusen has termed the "actual". (Van Dusen, 1975)

3. Awareness of awareness

This bridging process of consciousness in quantum physics is important in linking the potential applications of relativistic quantum field theory to Gestalt therapy.

Consciousness, awareness and observation are now at the heart of quantum physics. In trying to decide at what point quantum reality "collapses" into classical Newtonian reality of our senses, the key process is observation and awareness. In essence, the quantum world is subtle and the ultimate ground of existence out of which the classical world arises and becomes manifest and *relatively* autonomous through awareness. It is like a figure which emerges from the ground in a seemingly permanent way, like our own consciousness. Awareness plays an important role in joining these two rather contradictory views of reality - matter and field. As Bohm states -

"From this it follows that we are directly aware of the particle aspect of the universe through our senses and that the more subtle wave function aspect is inferred by thought about our sensory

experiences in the domain that is manifest to the senses."

(Bohm 1993, p314)

Therefore the classical world of matter that our senses perceive is constantly made figural by our awareness of the more subtle ground of the field nature of reality. The figure/ground process is not only in operation with sensory data of the visible world, but with the subtle experience of the invisible world of the field. As Bohm describes it -

"The Quantum world observes itself and the quantum measurement is a manifesting process"

(Bohm 1993, pp179)

This important role of awareness in linking matter and field, manifest and subtle realty, highlights crucial functions of the therapist. As already predicted by gestalt therapists, awareness by and of itself has an effect on reality. Perhaps in our ability to be aware of bridging these two realities, field and matter, we are, in effect, instruments of the field?

Commentary to Relativistic Quantum Field Theory - Implications for Gestalt Therapy

(Response to the commentaries of Latner, J. and Meara, A. to O'Neill, B., *Post Relativistic Quantum Field Theory and Gestalt Therapy,* Gestalt Review, Vol 12, no 1, 2008)

"That we are in the midst of conflicting theories of existence is really a delight. We must find out what is true for ourselves to find the way in all this richness. Our existence thankfully is far from simple."
Van Dusen, 2001, page 130

Originally when I started training in physics in the early 1970's, I would not have understood the delight expressed by Wilson Van Dusen in the quotation above. Sciences such as physics strive to reduce the complexity of existence to observable laws and theories which are increasingly inclusive and parsimonious. There is thus a reflex to reduce conflict between theories, not thankfully rejoice "in all this richness".

Carl Jung (1927), in writing the psychological commentary to the Tibetan Book of the Dead, argues the state of mind needed to understand such paradoxical reality is not readily available in Western society. He believed this scientific need for an "either/or" classification of reality leads to a denial of paradox, in comparison to the more affirmative "both/and" acceptance of paradox in the East.

I found a degree of delight in reading both commentaries, first in that I wanted to foster discussion on the development of the field perspective in Gestalt therapy. Second, I now find myself "in the midst" of conflicting commentaries.

Latner, for example, affirms that ideas such as field theory in physics are not only about life at the subatomic particle level but are "full of meaning about the lives we lead and about psychotherapy." Meara asserts that this is fraught with difficulties, is about highly contrived situations at unimaginable small scales and that for him "The concept of interaction mediated by particles with quantised characteristics is difficult to relate to therapeutic experience and Gestalt therapy." He inexplicably critiques Einstein's lack of currency as if this is the physics on which the article is based. This is unfortunately confusing as Einstein is referred to solely in the historical development of field theory, while the article is inspired by the work of Bohm (1993), long after the Standard Model Meara refers to which was developed in the 1970's.

Neither of the commentaries address the clinical and theoretical implications of current post relativistic field conceptualisations in the article and the crucial role of awareness in this formulation. The importance of awareness in physics as explained by Bohm (1993) embraces the paradox of the field, and provides the very precision of interlocking ideas with the connotative richness wanted by Latner.

The divergent views of the commentators may be a result of the different approach each has taken to field theory. Latner offers the field as an inspiring, evocative idea which is best thought of as an attitude, while Meara attends to the reductionist complexities of particle physics, plunging headlong into the "seething soup". This leads to a broad view of the field by Latner, much as an artist might view a house, while Meara describes the bricks and the cement which hold the house together.

Both authors consider the construction or co-creation of experience (Meara) and reality (Latner), and Meara proposes a likely ontology lies within field theory, open systems theory and holism as a "background figure" in gestalt therapy. Contrary to Latner, he assumes an open system is equivalent to field theory, and that the concept of boundary *between* organism and environment in Perls, Hefferline and Goodman is the same as boundaries *around* units of study such as atoms, organs and groups. However in minimising the difference of the terms "between" and "around" he creates an epistemological confluence and lack of discrimination between field and systems theories.

This theoretical blurring of system and field by Meara is the main issue Latner criticised in his original article and stresses in this commentary - that the field is not a system. He describes the field poetically as "an encompassing pregnancy, a potentiality which become actual and takes a specific form out of contact" and this is strikingly similar to how Bohm describes the quantum world, which is the subtle and ultimate ground of existence out of which the classical world arises and becomes manifest and *relatively* autonomous (Bohm & Hiley, 1993).

The implications of this likeness still await further dialogue so, true to the challenge raised by Parlett (2005), we do not isolate within our relatively small arena of gestalt therapy.

For Latner, as with Bohm and Perls et al, it is contact which denotes identity (or form), yet this identity is one in which the basic elements are constantly forming and dissolving. This is contrary to Meara's description of the ideal equilibrium state of an isolated system with a solid boundary and the "near equilibrium" or "far from equilibrium" systems which require import and export of energy.

Latner does not enter discussion of the seminal influences of field theory, while Meara partially describes a more complex perspective eruditely presented by Staemmler (2006). Meara draws a comparison between Lewin and Smuts and their relation to Perls, Hefferline and Goodman, in what appears a competition as to which is "most aligned". He favours Lewin whose revolutionary legacy lives on, while accusing Smuts of contradicting himself through a teleological agenda, relegating him to a "footnote in history." This aspect of his commentary would benefit from comparison with Staemmler's article on the exegesis of the term "field" in Gestalt therapy.

Meara's commentary is principally

theoretical while Latner spends a significant amount of time linking a field attitude to how to proceed therapeutically, taking up the exciting and necessary challenge to link theory to practice. He describes the "Reality Fight" relating this to a person's sense of insecurity around their beliefs. He connects this insecure sense of self to a field description of confluence, which is less the blurring of differences and more the ability to enter another's reality.

I would like to extend this field concept of confluence to include our ability, as Jung describes, to enter into both aspects of a paradox – to hold a "both/and" perspective of our own ideas as well as those of others. As a practical example, in teaching field perspectives we show students those books of pictures that look like a jumbled chaos of colours from which, when they learn to soften and de-focus their gaze, a three dimensional image appears. The "trick" is to learn to look with "soft eyes" and out of chaos can appear harmony, with both "realities" being true for the observer.

In a similar way Bohm (1993) states the perceived classical world is a result of each mind, aware of only a small part of the whole. The illusory aspect is believing that this part IS the whole, as when we believe the jumble of colours is all there is, as that is all we are able to see. When the classical world is perceived as a facet, then there is no illusion. So as therapists, the ability to "soften" our gaze to perceive other realities simultaneously becomes important. In a similar way, the issues raised by Latner and Meara have their own validity within the frame of reference they arise from, depending on our gaze.

This article, the commentaries, and my response have provided a re-evaluation of the understanding of the field in Gestalt therapy. To paraphrase Laura Perls (1992), perhaps there are as many fields and field theories, as there are Gestalt therapists. Hopefully as we share these perspectives together we paradoxically unfold the greater wholeness of the field within each different perspective, and expand our choice and gaze as therapists.

Early clinical applications of the relativistic quantum field theory within gestalt therapy.

In this chapter we consider how quantum field theory might inform us as therapists. What follows are some preliminary possibilities offered to encourage further discussion and conceptualization.

1. Active Information and quantum fields - Group Experience

In the Double Slit Experiment previously described, the motion of the particle as it passes through a slit is determined by information in the quantum field as a whole, so there exists what is called "active information" in the quantum field. As the particle reaches certain points in front of the slits, it is "in-formed" to accelerate or decelerate accordingly, sometimes quite violently. (Bohm 1993, pp 37) So the information in the quantum field that accompanies a particle which has already passed through either slit is available to the particles as they pass through. This is a field phenomenon which in essence also explains non-locality.

These qualitatively new features of the quantum potential imply novel quantum wholeness where the behaviour of the particle may depend crucially on distant features of the environment. Further there exists information in the field as a whole which is accessible to individual particles and influences them. This has a startling yet observable implication when applied to groups and the gestalt concept of the group as a wider self or "whole", as in the quantum phenomenon.

We can paraphrase this as follows -

If the field (group) has already learned something, the particle (person) in the field will have its motion determined (make choices) from quantum fields that have already experienced the phenomenon (from the current group field which includes its previous experiences in which the person was not present).

Such information gives us a wider view of the group as a self not only in classical Newtonian reality of each person affecting each other in the immediate environment (as in systems theory), but presents the group as a whole phenomenon carrying active information.

Therefore changes in the field affect others, even when they are not present but later return to the group. So we can expect to influence more than our immediate environment when a greater "whole" exists.

I have witnessed Gestalt therapists live by this maxim, and recall one example at a conference where the wider community had split over a dispute. The therapist in a smaller process group began by saying if we are true to our principles we will accept that whatever work we do here will affect the wider field, and the group accepted this and worked with this in mind, not only for themselves but the community as a whole. To give him due credit, his therapist was Malcolm Parlett at our AAGT conference in New York. This intervention by Malcolm was fitting as it was an Experiment in Community building which indeed happened. Sheldrake's (2003) work on morphogenic biological fields supports this idea of both action at a distance (non-locality) and the whole phenomenon affected by the field including parts that are distant.

This equally applies to work with couples and families where the work with one or more person can affect the wider system or self of which they are a part.

2. The Effect is in the Form of the Field not the Intensity – Couples

An affect of quantum fields is an often overlooked phenomenon in which the affect in a field is not determined by its intensity but only by its form. This is so different in the classical reality where the affect, or ability to do work, is in direct relation to the available force. So for example to move a ship requires a great amount of energy. On the contrary in the quantum field, a very weak field can produce a full quantum effect as this is related solely to the form and not the intensity of the field. In many ways this is more like the affect of a radio signal telling a ship where to go, where the radio wave is not directly pushing or pulling the ship that it guides. (Bohm 1993, pp 37)

105

Action of the Quantum Potential depends only on form not magnitude and so effect may be dominant even when intensity is small. This implies strong non-local connection of distant particles and strong dependence on its general environmental context.

Let us now consider the direct application of this in couples counselling (although this applies equally well to groups, families and communities).

When a couple attend for counseling there are certain forms or patterns of interaction which can configure the field and direct the action. Probably the most notable of these in Gestalt therapy is what Lee has termed the Shame Cycle or Shame Driven Contact Styles (Lee, 2004).

In an Australian context, where shame is not so culturally worded, I have found it more acceptable to explain this to couples as a Blaming Cycle. The interesting phenomenon with couples that I have noted is that no matter what the intensity of the issue they are dealing with, the form of these blaming or shaming cycles has the same affect. As in physics, it goes against common sense and intuition to believe that a low intensity issue, such as sanding a floor or even buying a box of tissues would have as strong affect on the couple.

However, once the *form* of the typical contact style/blaming cycle begins, no matter what the issue, the couple can precipitate an argument and feel as hurt over the box of tissues as over the deep betrayal of trust. The deeper issue can bring its own hue to the field and this also will colour the field. At the same time a couple can learn to trust and heal over little issues as much as big issues. The main implication we can gather is to notice the *form* and watch for changes in the *form* of contact style and not solely the *intensity* of the issue we are dealing with.

3. Passive and Active Information and Structured Ground

Bohm also talks of passive and active information which influences the field and the behaviour of the particle. He considers the literal meaning of information is to be 'in-formed', which is actively to put form into something or imbue it with form. (Bohm, 1993 pg 35) He considers how processes such as radio waves are *potentially* active everywhere and become active when it can give form to electrical energy. Other structures which exist as principally passive information are computer chips which hold so much information and even DNA.

This idea of passive information that

precipitates active information and then has an affect is strikingly similar and sympathetic of Wheeler's idea of Structured Ground which has been critiqued by some schools of gestalt therapy.

So these new scientific theories tell us that if the group has already learned something, the person in the field will make choices from fields that have already experienced the phenomenon (e.g. from the current group field which includes its previous experiences in which the person was not present). This is a structuring of the ground not only passively but actively as a process which provides information and directs action.

As therapists we can first attune ourselves to or be aware of these active and passive processes of information in the field (patterns); then feedback these patterns to the group, couple, family or individual; and finally offer experiments with these patterns.

Knowing that active and passive forms of information exist in the field support our work as therapists to look to the wider patterns of the "group as a whole" and notice what happens as passive or "implicit" patterns are made active or "explicit". In many ways the reality of quantum physics, simply supports what we already know as Gestalt therapists, yet adds a supportive space to encourage more dialogue with physics and physicists to discover deeper connections. These examples are simple mainly to encourage further dialogue and interest and build on the work of others such as Parlett and Bohm.

Conclusion

Relativistic quantum field theory presents a view of reality and self closely akin to that of

Gestalt therapy, to the seminal text of Perls, Hefferline and Goodman. As Bohm points out, rather than consider the differences between quantum theory and relativity, a clue to their convergence maybe found in their commonality. The key element their share in common is unbroken wholeness.

Echoing the writing of Smuts and Perls, Hefferline and Goodman, Bohm states -

"The forces between particles depend on the wave function of the whole system, so that we have what we may call 'indivisible wholeness'... Thus there is a kind of objective wholeness, reminiscent of the organic wholeness of a living being, in which the very nature of each part depends on the whole."

(Bohm,1993, pg 177)

This is strikingly similar to Perls, Hefferline and Goodman stating -

"The greatest value in the Gestalt approach perhaps lies in the insight that the whole determines the parts..."

(Perls, Hefferline and Goodman, 1951, pg xi)

This encourages us as therapists to move beyond the individual, reductionist nature of current psychology which sees only the separate therapist and client. This is encouragement to take the step of being aware of the "self" of the therapist/client, the "self" of the couple, of the 'self' of the group and of the community. Such a perspective supports us to see patterns of these larger wholes at work, patterns of homeostasis, polarization and growth. We can view this via the cycle of awareness or the Contact Episode (Polsters 1973) as a map to the active information processes underlying the apparent chaos of these aggregates.

So as we stretch our awareness to these

larger selves of couples, families and groups we enter quantum physics. Interestingly in Bohm and as in Perls, Hefferline and Goodman, it is contact which denotes identity and this identity is one in which the basic elements are constantly forming and dissolving in succession.

Finally, Gestalt therapists, in the challenge proposed by Parlett, can bring the needed framework and method to provide more than a reductionist "cure" for societies and individual ills. For it is through field theory, as originally expressed in Perls, Hefferline and Goodman, that we are encouraged to realize the impact of a life lived, not only in therapy sessions in a room, but in the way we teach, live and effect the wider field. There is a tension to simply be private practitioners in Gestalt therapy and let this become simply another modality of therapy. Or we can take up and live the challenge of our founders and be agents of growth, change and radical development in our society at large.

In the state of the world today, we clearly need more of both, in particular the latter.

Field Theory of the Couple: Poetry, Spirituality and Physics Meet
(Note: This chapter derives from work with my wife Jenny, and due credit is given)

Gestalt therapy is a distinctive paradigm from which to view the person and the couple. While more has been written recently it is the original text of Perls, Hefferleine and Goodman which offers a startling and vibrant description of the 'self'. The field is all there is, and as a clear figure which emerges from the ground, the organism is always part of this field and is defined by the field. Hence the definition of self is as follows:

> *"The self is a system of contacts in the organism/environment field".*

(Perls et al, 1951: 228)

In a manner which goes to the heart of the mystical writings describing the experience of self, the self is seen as indistinguishable and *at one* with the all that is.

"Let us call this interacting of organism and environment in any function the 'organism/environment field'; and let us remember no matter how we theorize about impulses, drives etc., it is always to such an interacting field that we are referring, and not to an isolated animal. Where the organism is mobile in a great field and has a complicate internal structure, like an animal, it seems plausible to speak of it by itself - as, for instance, the skin and what is contained in it - but this simply an illusion due to the fact that the motion through space and the internal detail call attention to themselves against the relative stability and simplicity of the background"

(Perls, Hefferline and Goodman,

1951 pg 228)

The implication of what is being said is stark and challenging -

Our sense of a separate self is an appearance or an illusion.

An illusion or at best an experience of self build on the functioning a separate ego which develops later. As the child starts to discriminate self and not self, such ego functions develop. As the child learns to language reality, this language of self and ego becomes the personality - the way in which we describe ourselves in words and ideas.

This definition of self in Perls, Hefferline and Goodman allows us to move beyond the separateness of ego to experience the many selves which arise, come into being and then fade into the ground. From this definition of self we can say that when two or more people become systematised in their contact with each other, they are a 'self', a couple. This idea is described originally in Gestalt psychology and the relationship to

117

the later work of Perls, Hefferline and Goodman is clear. The fundamental formula for Gestalt theory, as outlined by Wertheimer (1938) presents a description of the field and the self in a way which is consistent with the work of both Smuts and Perls, Hefferleine and Goodman.

> *"There are wholes, the behavior of which is not determined by that of their individual elements, but where the part-processes are themselves determined by the intrinsic nature of the whole"*
> *(Wertheimer, 1925 in Ellis 1938, pg 2)*

The connection to the later theory of Gestalt therapy is consistent. The organism is part of a larger field of organism and environment. In a statement predating the concept of self in Gestalt therapy, he describes the, functioning whole of a group of people, such as children or South Sea Islanders. In such the "I" rarely stands out

118

alone and it is the wider organism of the group which exists.

The Couple as One.

As we described earlier, the couple existing as a 'self' in the organism/environment field offers a unique way to work with a couple in therapy. In essence we realize the couple we are contacting is 'One Life'. They appear as two people of course, but in the view of the couple as one, a richer fuller tapestry emerges. This is at the heart of the original work by Martin Buber, I-Thou, and provides a lens with which to understand his deeply mystical and personal style of writing. As Buber writes -

> "The human being is not a He or She, bounded from every other He or She, a specific point in space and time within the net of the world; nor is he a nature able to be experienced and described, a loose

bundle of named qualities. But with no neighbour and whole in himself, he is Thou and fills the universe."

(Buber, 1958, pg 8)

While describing the separate person as 'whole in himself' (an individual), Buber paradoxically states he is a 'Thou' which fills the universe. The person is both a separate identity *and* connected to all of creation. Her separate identity also fills the universe and this is more than the individual personal nature of "self". This is experienced enduringly as part of a couple.

"By the very recognition that there is something larger present in the therapy situation than just the sum of the total of the individuals physically there, this is already a recognition of the more than personal"

(Hycner, pg 97).

This description is relevant to the couple, where there is indeed something "larger" present in the therapy situation than the sum of the two individuals physically present. There is a presence of that which is "more than the personal" - the couple self. Hycner describes the Hasidic story of the holy sparks, which are separated and contained in all, yet of the common source of wholeness.

To paraphrase this, the self as a couple (containing the holy sparks), is both two separate beings (sparks) nonetheless connected in the experience of coupling (wholeness). It is this connection we experience as the "between". We want to highlight this is a view of the couple *both* as a "oneness" (a self) and as two individuals in a field. As we experience the couple as a constant "self" then a wider view opens to therapy and spiritual life.

The Spiritual Life of the Couple as One

All religions in some form honor the spiritual nature of the couple. This sacred of coupling is described in the writing of Kahlil Gibran -

"You were born together, and together you shall be forever more,
You shall be together when the white wings of death scatter your days,
Aye, you shall be together even in the silent memory of God.
But let there be spaces in your togetherness.
And let the winds of the heavens dance between you."

The Prophet
Kahlil Gibran

Gibran in these lines describes the essence of a struggle that in constant in all couples work - the challenge to allow "spaces in your togetherness". This experience of "oneness" of the couple can challenge the experience of our separate sense of self. For a while we may tolerate the oneness in love making or in intimate states of looking after each other as a couple. Yet in such union there is also a heightened potential loss of ego control. This challenge to our experience of a separate, individual self may cause us to rebel and struggle as we enter the developmental processes of coupling. As Erv and Miriam Polster state -

"Contact is not just togetherness or joining. It can only happen between separate beings always requiring independence and always risking capture in the union. At the moment of union, one's fullest sense of his person is swept along into a new creation. I am no longer only me, but me and thee make we."

Gestalt Therapy Integrated
Polster and Polster, page 99

The couple is the new creation and the Polsters describe the challenge of risking capture in the union, gambling with dissolving individuality and wagering our independent existence. This attention to both the individual and couple experiences of self, and the tension between each is, to us as therapists, important. It is well explained through shame theory and the field theory definition of the couple.

When people reach the stage of their lives that they start looking for a partner, they have amassed various amounts of what Robert Lee calls ground shame and have developed creative adjustments that incorporate their ground shame into styles of connecting (Lee, 2008)).

Here is where a couple's "oneness" or "self" provides a lens that offers a unique view. This mix of life experience and beliefs as well as the individual's need for connection become an integral part of their couple "oneness." In this way a couple's "oneness" includes their mutual sense of disconnection as well as their longing for and amassed skills of connection.

As connection is the reason for coupling, connection and a wish to grow are the major driving forces performing in couples developing "oneness." However, in their "oneness," couples can find themselves moving toward connection OR they can find themselves reinforcing in each other the sense that connection is not possible. This is because, ironically, moving toward connection may activate the couples sense of the need of disconnection, to the extent the couple's joint underlying beliefs, embodied in their styles of connecting, contain taboos that need a disowning of certain aspects of self to "belong."

The degree to which a couple individually

"disown" aspects of themselves in order to be a couple, is a benchmark of the degree to which a couple may seek support and therapy to re-align these creative adjustments to become more authentic as a couple and as individuals.

Such experiences are paradoxical as is the change that is engendered and it helps to know at some level that this couple is a self. This offers the awareness for therapists not only of each individual but to the couple as a whole. This 'knowingness' can lead us to understand that there are two "realities" at play here - the reality obvious to our senses of the two people and the more subtle reality of the self of the couple. Each has a clear aesthetic to our senses, yet our phenomenological perspective needs to be developed to look for the signs of two individuals acting also as a couple. This is found in glances, in touch and in words, yet the phenomenological mind set which is only fixed to see the separate self of the individual will be "blind" to these sensory figures - to all intents and purposes this reality of the couple self is "invisible".

As we become aware this other reality exists, we can begin to relate to the couple "self" as well as the two individual selves which are present. We may ask the couple questions and look at what the couple do in physical space.

We may see the couple come in and say they are both nervous to be here and yet desperate and so are here nonetheless. They might be sitting far apart.

One person may say eventually

"the problem we are here with is that you hurt me being with another."

The other may say

"I didn't mean to and you never listened to me."

They may move further apart. They might say -

"you hurt me and I don't want to be with you anymore, I cannot trust you"

And the other person may say -

"I am bloody angry with you... how long do you want me to suffer for this, I just feel like leaving you again."

As each individual expresses these polarities of contact and withdrawal, we may start to notice paradoxically the couple itself has moved much closer physically and emotionally and is in full contact and not about to even consider leaving the room at this point. So we as therapists become aware there is a couple "self" here in the room. As we work from this awareness we may start to ask simple questions of the couple *as a whole* and not just each individual, such as -

"what moves you apart here as a couple and what brings you closer together?"

It is in such contact with the couple as a "self" the therapist begins to engage in couples work, and not only works with the two individuals as a couple, but also the couple 'as a whole". This allows for a new dimension of work to enter the therapy, as the impact of the couple on the individuals is also considered, and not only the sum of the individuals themselves.

The shift to a profoundly simple process of working with each individual and the couple as a 'whole' is not only a theoretical model. This is a lived reality which challenges our idea of being a separate self. The experience

129

of being a couple contrasts with the appearance of the separate selves, divorced from the wider field. This state of reality may be frightening to many, as we may feel we are losing our selves, risking capture in the union, as the Polsters described it. As poets, mystics, musicians and artists will testify, this is not an easy state to preserve. And as a minister once told us - "marriage is like your relationship with God - we struggle to get closer".

"There are wholes, the behavior of which is not determined by that of their individual elements, but where the part-processes are themselves determined by the intrinsic nature of the whole"

(Wertheimer, 1925 in Ellis 1938, pg 2)

There is the couple, the behavior of which is not determined by that of the two individuals that make up the couple, but where the individuals themselves are determined by the intrinsic nature of the couple.

The Way Our Theoretical Principles Inform Our Practice…

There is a practical interest in seeing the couple as an organism *in itself* as well as attending to each person. Having considered the various field perspectives of the couple, let's consider in what way these theoretical principles inform and direct work with couples. For example if we ascribe to only to one model (ie that the couple is a whole, an organism, a self) this can prematurely effect the therapy process of the individuals and highlight only the reality of the couple at the cost of neglecting the individuals who make up the couple.

There are times for instance when the couple are not ready to be received as a couple and share this intimacy and may be more aware of their individuality. In such instances the couple want to be attended to individually and this is so at the beginning of therapy. Each person has a sense of their issues, their hurts and their sense of shame and distress. When this is potent the couple may need individual therapy at the same time as the couples work to gain support or may even need to consider individual work first before coming together in the couples work.

As an example, with one couple recently they were being encouraged to experience their awareness as a couple and to work on the issues as a couple but they insisted, gently at first and then more strongly, the issues from previous marriages needed to be worked on separately. They saw these were individual issues which were getting in the way and they wanted the separate space to deal with this so as not to make this blurred with how they were as a couple.

Some theorists might argue against this approach and say that these issues are connected, yet this would not be hearing the couples need. At the very least we can be willing to experiment with the couple to find out what works and to take our lead from them. Sometimes the couples we have worked with have such a high degree of distress such as sexual abuse or domestic violence that individual work seems clearly signaled before working as a couple, yet in other cases couples are ready and mature enough as a couple to work on these issues together.

Deciding whether we focus the work with the couple on two separate individuals, OR whether we work with the couple as a self, would be best judged by the couple themselves. It is perhaps more the role of the therapist to be able to hold various models of couples and field theories to match these to the stage and pace of the couple when they come for therapy. As therapists we can learn to be able to shift our model and experience of reality to match that of the couple.

Gestalt therapists who approach couples work for the first time may be uncertain how to hold and work with these different "realities" The therapist will see clearly two separate people, in fact two people who seem *very* separate at times - so much so because they differ so much and may be about to separate.

To look at two people in couples work and see that they are also a gestalt - a whole - a self, is at times almost the opposite experience for the therapist - like being asked to believe the world is round when standing in the middle of a vast open plain.

The USE of the theory linked to the experience of being a therapist is this *knowingness* from our theory, as well as the knowingness from our lived experience as a couple, confirms we are also working with the reality of the couple as a "oneness". We know at some level this couple is a self. Just knowing this orients us to the couple as a whole.

For example it is easy to see the different polarities and contact episodes which start to play out for each individual - such as -

Person 1
"I want to get close to you but I am feeling vulnerable and want to protect myself ".

Person 2
"I am hurt and angry and want to protect myself but I also want to hurt you too for what you've done".

For the couple this becomes -

"I want to get close to you AND want to protect myself and be separate...

Or paradoxically for the couple this translates as -

"I want to get close to you and hurt you AND I am hurt and vulnerable and want to protect myself ".

This statement of theme of the Contact Episode (Polster and Polster 1973) is easy to see and read for the couple. The need (want to get close to you) is in counterpoint to the other need (I want to protect myself) and as the couple stay stuck with such strong polarities in the field they experience an impasse. Eventually they may come to therapy or creatively adjust and drink and do drugs, get depressed or have an affair. As we become more experienced in staying with the couple reality, as well as that of the two individuals, we can be aware of paradoxical

136

polarities in this dance of connecting and disconnecting, of shame and belonging. It helps as a couple to have experienced, talked about and understood theoretically, the polarity of wanting belonging which involves closeness, hurt and anger WHILE needing to disconnect through shame and vulnerability. This perspective of the couple oneness allows for a new dimension of work to enter the therapy. The impact of *the couple* on the individuals can be considered, and this is, in our view, a important element of the work.

We can work experience of "couple-ness" through simple phenomenological questions such as:

"what's it like to experience your selves as a couple and not just two separate people?"

Dialogically we can make statements about how we see them as separate people and how we experience them as a oneness, a couple. We can also dialogically share our own experience of being a couple. Further, there is an openness to experiment with this experience of being a couple and two separate people through experiences which present in the therapy room. With one couple who came in it was clear they were in tune with their separate individual natures and so we asked if they were metaphorically sitting on the sofa or two separate chairs today. They laughed and said they were sitting on the chairs and this became a useful reference to language the field of the couple and the individual selves.

Paradoxically, this focus on the couple can and does bring out the individual resistance to being a couple. This risk of losing individual "self" in the union of the couple "self" also highlights the subtleness of working with these individual and couple realities.

For 'first time' couple therapists it may be difficult to shift from the individual paradigm to a focus on the couple as a "oneness," because individual personalities are what our culture celebrates. To look at two people in couples work and see that they are also a gestalt - a whole (a self, is at times almost the opposite experience for the therapist - like being asked to believe the world is round when standing in the middle of a vast open plain.

As we become more experienced in staying with the couple reality, as well as that of the two individuals, we may be aware of paradoxical polarities in this dance of connecting and disconnecting, of shame and belonging. It helps as a couple to have experienced the polarity of wanting to belong *while* needing to disconnect through shame. This is so when our sense of vulnerability does not include the possibility of connection.

In therapy we find there are times when we are interested in working with both people and the couple as a whole, and other times when the focus is with one of the individuals in the couple and the other withdraws more into the background and attends. This offers the possibility for the therapist to work for a session with one of the people in the couple on family of origin issues, with the other present. This helps them to appreciate the beginning of these shame cycles and contact styles. This further confirms our understanding of the usefulness of at times working first with the individual process of one of the couple so they can, as a couple, come to understand and support each other better. Working this way allows the individual work to stay in the context of the couple, and like quantum physics allow the classical (individual) and couple (quantum) reality to inform our work as therapists.

Gestalt Family Therapy – A Field Perspective

(Note: This chapter derives from work with my colleague Seán Gaffney, and due credit is given)

Abstract

Surprisingly little attention has been given to the gestalt approach to family therapy. Where this has happened it has either reformulated it with systems theory or described a unique perspective of a practitioner. With recent trends in gestalt therapy in developing the field perspective, closely akin to systems theory, it is now timely to consider how gestalt therapy can be clearly explained as a theory of practice to working with families. This chapter outlines the work of the therapist as being field sensitive, insightful, affective and present, and offers subtle yet key practices which define the field perspective, adding a dimension to the gestalt approach with families, yet to be more fully explored.

Family therapy has developed as a specific form of therapy which works with the family as a whole, as well as individual members. It is a therapy, or grouping of therapies, based mainly on systems theory and the application of cybernetics.

There are significant likenesses between the worldviews of family therapy and gestalt therapy and it is at first surprising that more has not been written about Gestalt family therapy. What restricted the application of gestalt therapy in working with families is the skewed development of gestalt therapy itself. While it began as a field perspective gestalt therapy shifted to an individualist, clinical practice (Wheeler, 2000) even in the application to groups (O'Neill & O'Neill, 2008.) This ironically resulted in authors suggesting how to bridge the *individualistic* paradigm of gestalt therapy to systems theory (Armstrong, 1988; Zinker, 1994; Lynch & Lynch, 2005).

The challenge linking the gestalt approach to family therapy and to systems theory is preserving the uniqueness of the gestalt approach and its core principles of practice. This is difficult when family therapy has a well established, strong theory base which overshadowed the uniqueness of gestalt therapy in the literature. Indeed some of the writing in gestalt family therapy presents it as *an adjunct* to the family therapy approach, or *an amalgam* (Zinker, 1994; Lynch & Lynch 2005), rather than a unique application of the principles of gestalt therapy to working with families. Others such as Kempler (1974) developed their unique theory of gestalt family therapy based on their practice, with little if any emphasis on current theory such as dialogue and the field perspective.

This processes of amalgamation of the gestalt therapy with systems theory has arisen, it can be argued, because a theory of

143

practice of gestalt therapy field perspective was absent. What has been described as contemporary gestalt the last decade or so is an articulation of the field and dialogical perspectives and refining field theory in linking theory to practice (Latner,1983; Yontef, 1993; Parlett,2005; Staemmler, 2006; O'Neill & Gaffney, 2008).

These developments in gestalt therapy pave the way to apply and explain a theory of practice of gestalt family therapy, which builds on the current field perspective writing. This is supported by increasing numbers of gestalt therapists extending beyond individualist practice and working with couples, families, groups and organizations.

It is of particular note that Philippson (2005) describes a perspective of gestalt family therapy based not on systems theory as an amalgam, but based solely on his conceptualization of field theory from Perls, Hefferline and Goodman. Importantly, as well as noting the likenesses between these two approaches, Philippson highlights the differences between systems theory and field theory. This is becoming increasingly more important as these differences are essential to maintaining the principles informing Gestalt therapy practice.

Understanding what works in family therapy – the importance of our worldview

There is much that has been written about family therapy from other modalities, particularly systems theory, and much that has been researched. Simons (2006) argues the literature of family therapy finds itself still unable to answer the critical question of what makes family therapy work. He notes –

"The two dominant approaches to answering this question, the common-factors perspective and the model specific factors perspective, remain divided at this juncture by a fundamental difference of emphasis between the two. "

(Simons, 2006, pg 331).

He proposes a way of integrating these two perspectives is through the theory the therapists achieve maximum effectiveness by committing themselves to a family therapy model of proven efficacy whose underlying worldview closely matches their personal worldview.

This co-created process of worldview and principles matching the lived practice of the therapist is in keeping with research on outcome studies, in areas such as domestic violence. Current research in domestic and family violence suggests the relationship between the therapist and client system is chief and is affected by the lens of the therapist (Alexander, & Morris, 2008; Musser, Semiatin, Taft, & Murphy, 2008; Levesque, Driskell, Prochaska, & Prochaska, 2008; Murphy, & Maiuro, 2008). In this context of co-creation a clearer application of the developments in the gestalt field perspective to family therapy is timely as such ideas are central to the principles of gestalt therapy.

The Field Perspective in Gestalt Family Therapy

The seminal text (Perls, Hefferline and Goodman,1951) did not describe a field *theory* but an ontological statement about reality – the field is real. This is in accord with similar writing in physics, where the field was at first viewed as a model or representation, and was then declared to be real with Maxwell's four equations of the electromagnetic field (Einstein & Infield, 1931; Bohm, 1993; O'Neill, 2008).

An alternative field perspective in gestalt therapy has been based on the work of Lewin (1936) which describes the field as a theoretical epistemology, a *method* for understanding reality but not the reality itself – like a map – or as Lewin termed it similar to a handicraft.

In our current writing (O'Neill & Gaffney, 2008) we have stressed that each of these perspectives are valid and useful to inform practice. We gathered the main commonalities and presented them as a field perspective, outlining the principles and practices which accord with both approaches and present a more unified and practical approach to field theory. The following section outlines theoretical precepts which describe the principles of the field perspective and their application to family therapy. It begins by outlining the principles of an integrative perspective, followed then by family therapy practices which flow from these principles.

Principles of Gestalt Family Therapy from a Field Perspective

The interlocking theoretical principles which inform and guide the work of gestalt therapists in working with families and that describe the attitudes and practices used in the field perspective are defined by O'Neill and Gaffney (2008). What follows is a brief review of these principles and how they relate to gestalt family therapy.

Principle – The Self as Process

Gestalt therapy described the person as a fluid part of an organism/environment field. This does not lessen the sense of separateness experienced by each person but contextualizes the experience of self within a wider field. As stated in the seminal text –

"The self is a system of contacts in the organism/environment field"

(Perls et al, 1951: 228)

More importantly for gestalt family therapy, this theoretical perspective describes larger "selves" or organisms, similar to a biologist who may study a bee hive and not just the bee. Therefore when two or more people become systematized in their contact with each other, they are a *self* from a gestalt perspective. When a couple birth a child the self of the family is also born and with that a wider, more complex system of contacts in the field.

Principle – The Whole Determines the Parts

This principle accords with principles in systems theory in family therapy. The subtle difference (which also carries through to practice), is that systems theory focuses on the dynamics *between* the people in the system, compared to the field perspective which *works with the family as a whole*, as an entity in itself . To stereotype models in this way is purely a convenience to gain a sense of the difference between perspectives. We accept that therapists may work and act with families from various perspectives at the same time. Systems theory does describe well the impact of the system on the individuals in the family.

The additional aspect of the gestalt perspective is to view the family as a "self" with *agency* as a "self". This is not different to where the current wave of family therapy is today, however from this perspective the gestalt approach offers ways of being with and a part of the wider "self" of the family plus therapist.

Principle – The Parts Determine the Whole

As a mirror of the previous principle, this principle expresses the importance of the elements on the whole, the impact of each family member on the overall family. This includes the awareness, dialogue and movement between individual people and the family as a whole. The focus is therefore on the relationship between the whole and the elements or what systems theory calls sub systems (parents, adults, partners, children and individuals).

There are times when for example the therapist will attend to the importance of the singularity and uniqueness of the person, while at other times noting the relationship of the individual to the family or sub systems. This movement between the individual, sub systems and family is a choice of the therapist and there are times when the needs of the individual outweigh the needs of the family or sub system and other times when the family or sub system needs outweigh those of the individual.

Principle – The Wisdom of the Organism

In seeing the family as an organism, a self, carries the premise that such an organism has an inbuilt wisdom, just like any other self or organism. Gestalt therapy sees the figure /ground formation (when allowed to act unobstructed) as an organic process which looks after the immediate needs of the organism. Families come to therapy with this figure/ground flow of the organism decreased in some way – fixed gestalten and redundant creative adjustments – and therefore the work of the therapist is to aid the family to access their homeostatic and growth processes. This principle is articulated by Zinker (1994) and Lynch & Lynch (2005) as being in keeping with a blended gestalt and systemic approach.

While they note there are differences in style of how this principle is applied, there is also space for creative intervention and direction by the therapist, as the therapist is also now part of the family system.

Principle – Paradoxical Agency

Paradoxical agency from the stance of the therapist is a key attitude of the gestalt approach to family therapy. After teaching gestalt therapy for over three decades perhaps the biggest challenge in learning this approach, is the student/therapist not trying to control and influence the therapy process and instead allowing and being in a therapeutic space of being present, aware and responsive in the field. This is a paradoxical process of searching for balance between choice and acceptance and is described in the original text of Perls, Hefferline and Goodman as the "middle mode" - the space between active and passive functioning, where the person is accepting, attending and growing into the solution, and the substitution of readiness (or faith) for the security of apparent control (Perls, Hefferline and Goodman, 1951).

Principle – The Needs Organises the Field

Perls et al. (1951) described two prime needs of the organism to be those of *growth* and *homeostasis*. Lewin added to this how the phenomenology of the organism also plays a part in how the field is perceived. Therefore a clump of trees in a field is seen as needing to be removed by a farmer, used as shelter by a soldier and a place for romance by a couple.

The gestalt therapist may note that while each individual in the process has their own individual needs (love, attention etc) these may not be the need of the family as a whole (i.e. mother attending to baby, adult

155

children leaving home etc.). Being able to have bi-focal lens and note the patterns of individual and family process allows the therapist to work not only with the individuals and the relationships between them, but the family as a whole. From this awareness the family and its members can now choose and allow processes of the family organism of which they are a part, as well as the individuals in their own life space.

Principle – Harmony within Chaos: Nothing Unconnected Ever Happens

The field perspective asks the therapist to be aware of the process by which the family and its members 'pattern' or make sense of what is figural for them. Often what is brought to therapy is the struggle of any organism to understand conflicting figures, such as love and hate, or attachment and need for separateness. Being attuned to and aware of these patterns of contact supports therapists to make sense of what appears paradoxical and self defeating behaviors, and understand families are doing what they do from some need to creatively adjust to the environment. Parlett (2005) states that as gestalt therapists we know that much of what seems inconsequential is organised; it is meaningful in some context of which we may be partially or completely unaware. These patterns are 'harmonics' within the seeming chaos of the family. They underlie the initial problem of the family. These are the patterns of contact which develop when the environment is not meeting needs and the family must adjust creatively. From this principle the stance of a gestalt therapist is one of a phenomenological attunement to the organising patterns of the family, the individuals and other selves (such as the couple, parent and child sub-systems.)

Gestalt Family Therapy - A Theory of Practice

The next section outlines the way in which a gestalt therapist, working from a contemporary field perspective, is guided to use these principles in the practice of family therapy.

The Genesis of the Family

The gestalt therapy field perspective offers the therapist a lens to view the life of a family and the challenges each stage of life brings. Today there are multiple variants of the traditional family, including single parent families, same sex parent families, step families, blended families and separated parent families. So much so a household of two originally partnered people with their own children is close to becoming a fringe group. However for the sake of parsimony we will describe the traditional process of family development of a couple who decide to have a child. From a field perspective the 'self' of the family first arises when a child becomes part of the parent system – in other words when the couple decides to have a baby. (I will use the terms of 'mother' and 'father' for convenience knowing same sex parents will also experience these same processes) The identity of the mother and father start changing as they anticipate becoming "parents". Similarly the identity of the couple begins to change as the couple now becomes a "family". Even after the child is born, the couple is still the figural "self" in the household – the "couple" have a child. Yet the impact of this on the identity of the "couple" becomes clear and the arrival of another individual into the household brings a field where other 'selves' become more figural. This includes the "mother-child" self, and the "father-child" self as well as the "mother-father-child" self, or family.

This development of a couple into a family creates heightened attachment and belonging (there are more selves to be part of) and paradoxically more potential for loss of attachment and a sense of isolation (there are more sub groups I may not belong to).

The Work of the Therapist

Families, in whatever form they take, either decide or are referred to a family therapist because one or more of the people in the family are experiencing some form of disorder. This is also obviously connected to processes within the family as a whole which cause the individual to seek help.

Much of what a family brings to therapy is initially hidden or implicit. The work of the therapist is be aware of the experience of these implicit realities of the field of the family, how they manifest for the therapist in their own felt experience and imagery, as well as the figure ground formation of client and therapist. In working as a phenomenologist the therapist attends to her own experience of self in the family/therapist field, noticing what the family and the individuals do.

Like a compass which is affected by and discloses "invisible" magnetic fields, the compass needles of the therapist's proprioceptive experience, imagery and figure ground formation are the guides in this more intimate setting of family therapy work. The work of the therapist is to be aware of, attend to and experiment with these rich figures which present.

There are four ways of being as a therapist which are practiced by Gestalt therapists and show that they are working from a Field Perspective (O'Neill & Gaffney, 2008). These are titled – Field Sensitive Practice; Field Insightful Practice; Field Affective Practice and the practice of being Field Present.

The following section will now explore these as they relate to family therapy from this current field perspective.

Field sensitive practice – Authentic Self as a Field Phenomenon

A field sensitive approach in practice is one in which the therapist attends how our sense of self is "field dependent". This is a sense of self found in whatever becomes figural, even though it may not at first seem organized or meaningful. This means trusting in the emerging figure, knowing that eventually patterns will emerge and that these will start, eventually, to make sense.

This is learning not to "force" a pattern or meaning, nor to try to work it out analytically or cognitively, but to allow meaning to emerge from the field and within a dialogue with the family. In the Life Space of the family we discover meaning in the way in which they individually and collectively organize their world and their sense of self and the important interplay between self and other.

For example if a child is having trouble with school, how does each member of the family and the family as a whole understand and react to this. One parent may sound understanding, another parent critical and a sibling may make jibes. There may be no clear meaning for the family as a whole. If we hear from the child that they are being bullied (for example) this may alter the meaning for the individuals and family as a whole – both parents may become sympathetic and outraged at the school and the sibling may want to stand up for their younger sibling. The family as a whole may display a solidarity and protection with the underlying meaning that "we might attack each other but no one may attack our family" etc.

As the phenomenology of one individual is understood (the child), the phenomenology of the family as whole can change and the meaning which separate the family now draw it together and start to emerge – a picture of how the family views the world and events that happen, particularly here and now.

Therefore with a field sensitive approach the therapist supports the individuals to shift from their own separate life spaces to a more connected and collective one, enabling each member to become more sensitive to the life space of the other. These individual shifts also bring about a shift for the family as a whole, creating a greater sense of solidarity and sensitivity to each others' life space.

Field insightful practice

The application of being field insightful is obvious when Gestalt therapists inquire about a wide field of influence and possibilities of meanings. This means keeping a fluid openness to the possible interconnection of people, events and situations. There is also giving relevance to each event as not random but ordered and to seek to make explicit this order by enquiry and experiment. In this way the gestalt therapist is constantly an action researcher, finding out the meaning and connections being made by the family through inquiry in an experimental cyclic fashion, much in the same way a systemic family therapist does.

Like physics, this attitude in Gestalt therapy is one which is *relativistic* and while a separate "reality" may exist, the person will always have a relative view of this within the field. Thus gestalt therapists will accept that while they may feel their view is the right one, there is space for the other view as part of a wider reality and even the possibility that they are simply wrong. This does not mean giving up one's view but realizing there are more or different views being held by others. As Parlett (2005) states, there is a willingness to address and explore the organized, interconnected, interdependent, interactive nature of complex human phenomena.

The various maps of Gestalt therapy previously mentioned are applicable at this point, and each person can express and experience the theme that is developing. Usually the theme is one in which polarities are in operation and shaping the field in the same way two magnets underneath a table shape a field of iron fillings on the table. Until we see the magnets we are unaware of their influence.

For example silence in a family, when explored, may happen when people are both angry and frightened. There are the polarities of fight or flight in operation. If members cannot express either of these we may witness a family with one or more members being depressed. As they can express either fear or anger safely, the link to depression becomes more obvious. They can then consciously choose to withdraw or voice anger instead of being together in a silent depressed state.

The work of the gestalt therapist is to aid the family to understand and experiment with these polarities so they do not become "fixed gestalten" which hold the family in a stuck place. By being able to become aware of the existence of polarities, such as fight or flight, the family can experiment with what might happen as first one and then the other polarity is acknowledged and expressed. Rather than a frozen silence the family can deal with how to express hurt or anger and support and protect themselves in the process.

Field affective practice

This practice is found in the presence of gestalt therapists supporting the family in experimentation. This leads to further enquiry discovering what happens as the context changes – in what way does the family change. The therapist encourages experimenting with themes such as exploring what might happen if one told another they were hurt as well as angry – what is this like?. This is guided by techniques of exaggeration/reversal and repetition/reformulation of polarities. The therapist themselves may offer how they see each person and/or the family as a whole and say how each person and the family affects them.

An example may be in how each family member tolerates the polarities of love and hate. A family that preserves a strong sense of love for each other but does not tolerate anger needs individual and collective creative adjustments to "deal with" anger. The therapist may share their own experience of this in the family and ask if this fits for others, or may say "I don't feel I could get annoyed in this family – does anyone else feels the same?"

Thus with the support of the therapist, the family have the opportunity to "be angry" or "be hurt" or "be loving" without needing to creatively adjust or take it outside of the family. Thus they finally find the closeness of the family paradoxically grows in allowing these frozen behaviors to melt. In other cases, where anger is present regularly, its polarity maybe that expression of hurt is disallowed. When hurt is allowed the field will once again change. This willingness to experiment is a key in field affective practice. It offers a possibility to both the therapist and the family to not stay stuck with repetitive cycles of behavior and explore different and freeing ways of being with each other.

The son and father who constantly end with the father angry and the son sullen may evolve as a family when the father risks telling the son he is also hurt and the son risks saying he also loves his father.

Field present practice

Finally a field perspective which is enfolded in the practice of Dialogical psychotherapy becomes a practice which is present, inclusive and committed to dialogue.

From the field perspective the therapist and family explore the experiences of having the therapist present in the intimate space of the family. As the family experience another person with them so that as well as the "family" there is the "family and therapist" the work becomes also about the dialogue that develops. This offers an experience by the family of another person who responds to them as a family in a way that is unique and relating to them. A simple question from the therapist such as "how do you imagine I see you and even feel about you as a family" is one of significant dialogical impact and needs the family to be in a place where they can integrate and trust such feedback from the therapist. This is where the therapist is part of the family/therapist field and also experienced by the family as an "other" – in dialogical terms as a "Thou". This offers the therapist a dialogical approach with individuals within the family and the family as a whole. For example if the therapist tells the child who is being bullied that they think they are brave to bring this into the family, this will affect the child, the parents, the other siblings and the family as a whole. A simple yet profound intervention from a gestalt perspective – being present with the family, including ourselves in the life of the family, being committed to be in dialogue with them and showing that how we are as therapists is something that is lived and not a technique or style of intervention alone. Such an approach to practice is detailed by the work of Martin Buber (1958)

Conclusion

The importance of developing the field perspective in gestalt therapy is in the support provided to teaching, supervision and practice of gestalt family therapy. The way of being a gestalt family therapist, being field sensitive, insightful, affective and present, offers subtle yet key practices which define the field perspective, and add a dimension to the gestalt approach with families. I believe this yet to be more fully explored and described.

At a philosophical and theoretical level, gestalt therapy and traditional family therapies can learn, parallel and synthesis together in the rich interchange which becomes possible as the fixed gestalts about each melts. In systems theory this is described as the change that happens as the dominant discourse of a system or family is altered when the hidden discourse emerges. The richness and similarities between systems theory and gestalt therapy offer more possibilities for cross fertilization and enrichment. Much of this has been missed so far because practitioners of both these approaches hold fixed, often outdated views of the other – this is now changing.

At a clinical practice level the gestalt therapist has much that can be offered in announcing the dialogical and experimental aspects of family therapy, while the phenomenological roots of gestalt therapy are in accord with family therapy ideas of discourse and hypothesis.

At a field perspective level, Gestalt therapists offer the potential exploration of the subtle movements in the paradoxical elements of therapist control and surrender, and the paradoxical control discovered through surrender. This is now apparent in the work and research developing with couples and families where violence, control and social control are figural. Particularly in Australia, gestalt therapy has offered a paradigm attuned to current literature and research, which allows for heightened engagement through attunement to client needs and the explication and lived reality of the authentic self. This not just a therapy, it is a subtle living of a field perspective practice as a way of life.

David Bohm: Quantum Physicist with Insights to Gestalt Therapy and Spirituality

"And the end of all our exploring
Will be to arrive where we started
And know the place for the first time.
Through the unknown remembered gate
When the last of earth left to discover
Is that which was the beginning;
At the source of the longest river
The voice of the hidden waterfall
And the children of the apple tree
Not known, because not looked for
But heard, half heard, in the stillness
Between two waves of the sea."

T.S. Eliot, "Little Gidding"

In the application of physics and quantum physics to psychotherapy there are other areas which support our understanding of psychotherapy and spirituality. In particular David Bohm (1993) in his book with B. J. Hiley *The Undivided Universe* offers understanding and metaphors from quantum physics which translate to both psychotherapy and spirituality. Bohm had worked with Einstein and became Professor of Theoretical Physics at London University. He made use of two related phenomenon in dealing with the limits of relativistic quantum theory.

First was the hologram, which produces a three-dimensional image by splitting and reunifying light and offers a model for both how the brain "creates" reality and each part of a reality contains the whole.

What interested Bohm was the hologram does not look like the object but creates an image when it is illuminated by a laser beam. From 'separate points of perspective' of Cartesian geometry, the hologram produces another order of wholeness, which he saw as "enfolded" or "implicit" within the form. So the hologram is enfolded and implicate order (invisble reality) and this can be unfolded to produce an explicate order (visible reality).

This process of enfoldment and unfoldment was seen by Bohm to match to the laws of quantum reality and the shifts between classical reality and quantum reality through awareness.

The second phenomenon which interested Bohm was an apparatus made of two concentric glass cylinders with a viscous liquid between the outer and inner cylinder. Into the fluid is put a drop of insoluble ink. When the cylinder is rotated the ink spreads out into a thread and eventually disappears.

However when the order is reversed and the cylinder rotated back the ink droplet reappears. Therefore while it looks like there is no visible order once it has disappeared, there is obviously, like the hologram, some order otherwise the droplet could not reform.

When a series of droplets are used then the order between them at first seems not to exist yet as they enfold and unfold it becomes clear they are linked in some way by an implicate order. This is similar to the particles in the Einstein, Podolsky, Rosen (EPR) experiment in which particles appear connected over large distances.

Bohm and Hiley (1993) state that an event thus is only "actual" or observable to us as it unfolds into manifest reality, yet it is always present whether unfolded or not. Bohm's holographic ontology extends beyond current relativistic quantum field theory to a process of the constant enfolding and unfolding of classical reality and quantum fields which he calls "holomovement". Therefore the world of the classical physics of our sensory apparatus (awareness and contact functions) unfolds out of the ground of quantum potential and so this movement (or holomovement) is a constant figure/ ground process as described in Gestalt therapy. Our ability to see beyond the jargon of each approach and hear the similarities offers a wider lens.

In short what is exciting about this to the non-scientist (particularly a Gestalt therapist) is that someone like Bohm is describing the awareness process of figure/ground and organism/environment field. However this is not clear at first as he is using quantum physics language and not psychotherapeutic language. This has been noted earlier in the same context of mystical and spiritual language with psychotherapy.

Manifest and Subtle, Explicate and Implicate orders – The role of the therapist

Applying this idea of holomovement to our work as therapists offers the proposition that a similar phenomenon happens in Couples therapy, for example. As we see couples affected by each other "as if" they were a single organism and at times we see the two individuals (classical or explicit reality) which is visible. Like the droplets visible (the two people we see) and then we are aware of the relationship itself (quantum or implicit reality) which is invisible yet nonetheless real.

This phenomenon is similar with groups where the individuals stand out and at times the group as a whole is more obvious. There are times when the implicit or invisible reality apparent within groups also figural, for instance when the missing member of the group has a presence and an effect on the group-as-a-whole. As a dear friend once said to me "Absence is presence."

The *Experience of Being Stared At* and *I - Thou* Reality

In our practice as therapists we are interested in both explicate and implicate orders of the field. The work of the therapist is to be aware of, connect with, and experiment with the constant unfolding and enfolding of the field. Such connections are also described by Sheldrake, a British biologist. He has described the ontological existence (reality) of what he terms "morphogenic filelds". In essence these biological fields are responsible for uniting biological matter. As he describes it, the DNA of mouse does not by itself create a mouse and needs the action of biological fields which "tell" the mouse to form from the DNA.

His research has extended to experiences of connection between people which propose the existence of similar biological fields which join people. These fields explain such experiences as knowing who is on the phone when it rings and the awareness of being stared at. He has researched these phenomena and argues they offer clear evidence for the existence of implicate biological fields of order which connect all life forms.

At a quantum level Bohm and others note that such connections are possible within the holomovement and that indeed rather than only one person affecting each other at a distance, each person, as with a hologram, contains the whole within them and hence is connected in ways we are still to discover. This is not unlike to the work of the poet and mystic William Blake when he writes:

"To see a world in a grain of sand,

And a heaven in a wild flower,

Hold infinity in the palm of your hand,

And eternity in an hour."

Auguries of Innocence

William Blake

Bohm's idea of implicate order and the holomovement, parallels the process of figure/ground in gestalt therapy theory of the self. He notes the idea of a permanent entity with a given identity (self) is at best an approximation (illusion) whether this be a particle or anything else. This is similar to writing in Perls, Hefferline and Goodman which states:

"Where the organism is mobile in a great field and has a complicated internal structure, like an animal, it seems believable to speak of it by itself–as, for instance, the skin and what is contained in it–but this is simply an illusion due to

the fact the motion through space and the internal detail call attention to themselves against the relative stability and simplicity of the background."

(Perls, Hefferline and Goodman

1951, 228)

The experience of separateness in experiencing the self is illusory, or at best built on functioning a separate ego-sense of self that develops later in early life. These physical and biological realities give credence to what is defined as a model or theory but not an ontological reality - the whole being more than the sum of the parts.

As Buber writes, again echoing this wider concept of identity of Bohm:

"The human being is not a He or She, bounded from every other He or She, a specific point in space and time within the net of the world; nor is he a nature able to be experienced and described, a

184

loose bundle of named qualities. But with
no neighbour and whole in himself, he is
Thou and fills the universe."

(Buber, 1958, pg 8)

So our ideas in Gestalt therapy that the group is a self and the couple is a self is supported by theories which explain physical and biological field conditions to make this possible. Further the connection between two people as they experience a sense of I - Thou and the "between" that exists can be described as as *the experience of the implicate order* which is not obvious in our awareness of the classical reality of separate self. Such an experience might also be said to be a direct awareness of morphogenic fields and the "ties that bind us".

As we begin this dialogue with science, the realities which are becoming uncovered by quantum physics and biology provide

185

assurance that field theory, which at first was put forward as ontological reality and later became more an epistemological tool, is supported and correlates with the current state of the sciences from which the early influence on Gestalt therapy arose.

Bohm's and Sheldrakes work has been taken up by many popular science writers such as Wilber and Capra as providing an explanation for phenomena such as transpersonal experiences, psychic phenomena, the Near Death Experience, and religious and mystical experiences. Wilber cautions against the premature extension of these theories in this way, yet clearly this dialogue has now begun and will continue

Such a resounding correlation with science supports our early psychology of wholeness and the organism/environment field of Perls, Hefferline and Goodman and the further work of many gestalt therapists. It encourages consideration of the trend to integrate and expand Gestalt therapy with the physical and spiritual domains of experience.

These physics and biology models can be considered for their application to Gestalt therapy. In what way is the understanding of holographic fields and holomovement able to influence theory and practice of psychotherapy. Recent writing in Gestalt therapy (Parlett, 2006, O'Neill, 2008) have extended the use of field theory to that of biology and physics, and propose the gestalt therapy conceptualization of the "self" is supported by theories which explain physical and biological field conditions. In developing this dialogue with science, the realities becoming uncovered by quantum physics and biology provide assurance the idea of "field, at first described as ontological reality (Perls, Heffereline and is supported and correlated with the current state of the sciences from which the first influence of field theory arose.

Rather than working within a reductionist client/therapist framework, from this integrative perspective Gestalt therapists, can develop a methodology to provide more than a simple reductionist "cure" for individual ills., We realise through a field perspective the impact of a life lived and shared which effects the wider field in body, mind and soul. This chapter explored the tension between the view of Gestalt therapy as another modality of therapy and a views which expands it into wider fields of operation. This maintains the challenge of the founders to be agents of growth, change and radical development in our society at large.

Einstein (1938) points out that science and particularly physics, is not just a collection of laws or facts – it is a creation of the human mind. The theories of physics are trying to form a picture of reality and link this to the world of sense impressions.

As Bohm pointed out, our theories are not forms of knowledge of the world but forms of insight into the deeper nature of reality as a whole. Bohm and Einstein note the important role of imagination in this process. It is an important nexus between that which is considered ontologically *real* and our experimental and mathematical methods which inform and interact with our consensus of what is indeed *real* by our senses. Therefore processes such as physical observation, mathematics, theoretical conceptualisation, prediction and experimentation all interact to create a view of our world.

While our sensory view may appear dominant, it is essentially only one view, and that of *appearances*. The physicist continually works to determine the *essence* of the appearances, and historically what happens is that which was once seen as *essence* later becomes a realised *appearance*. The world was flat and then round.

> "*Within the domain of such experience, it may be said that this world is manifest. According to its Latin root, the word manifest would signify what can be held in the hand*"
>
> (Bohm 1993, pg 176)

and also

> "*We may say that the quantum world is subtle.... It's root meaning is based on the Latin subtexlis which signifies 'finely woven'. Clearly the quantum world as we have described it cannot be held in the hand or any other way*'

Nevertheless we are proposing it is real and indeed that it constitutes a more basic reality than does the classic 'world'....it is an abstraction from the subtle quantum world which is being taken as the ultimate ground of existence."

(Bohm 1993, pg 177)

Appearance and Essence.

Bohm argues that appearances in sense perception give rise to inferences about an essence. No matter how far we go we are therefore involved in perception and not universal reality. Mathematics and sense perceptions are appearances which guides our action towards the unlimited and unknown reality. The ultimate nature of awareness is unlimited and unknown, like that of the universe of which it is a part. What then is the use of an ontological interpretation of quantum theory – it is because it reflects reality within its own domain. So although each form of thought about the essence is an appearance, it also reflects a reality that is always dependent for its existence as well as for its qualities on broader contexts and deeper levels. Here we discover the use of the hologram where each part or domain gives us information about the whole at the same time as being a part.

The Enfoldment and Unfolding of Reality

Finally for Bohm this is the inclusion and description of consciousness as a quantum phenomenon. He describes consciousness as a process unfolding and enfolding between the classical world and the quantum world - a bridge between both which is part particle or matter phenomenon and part quantum field effect. Bohm's holographic ontology extends beyond current quantum field theory in a process of the constant enfolding and unfolding of classical reality and quantum fields in a process he calls "holomovement".

This is remarkably similar to Swedenborg's description of this -

> "As this cannot come at once to the perception of the understanding or before being reduced to order and then unfolded and demonstrated according to that order, let this be the order in considering it"

(Swedenborg, 1768/1992, pg 198)

So the classical physics of our sensory apparatus unfolds out of the ground of quantum potential and this movement is a constant figure/ ground process in birthing our "self" through awareness. Our experience of self in Classical Reality is "birthed" from quantum reality, perhaps one day to return and there remain.

Addendum:

(This is provided as an expanded version of the physics described in this book for those who wish to read a little more on the topic)

Understanding Field Theory in Physics

The one idea that students struggle with most in Gestalt therapy is Field Theory. This short paper is offered as a way to better understand the impact and application of field theory in Physics. It is helpful to begin with an understanding of just how the terms "field" and "field theory" are being used in physics and in particular, to what extent are these terms used as an epistemology (that is for gaining and certifying knowledge) and second as an ontology (that is expressing the nature of being), with each term not exclusive of the other.

Field as representation and Field as Real in Physics

In physics Einstein and Infield (1938) state the most important development since those of Newton is - the field. The field is at first a way of representing vectors of force in a schematic drawing of forces such as gravity and it is purely a representation of reality. However with the arrival of Maxwell's equations describing the structure of the field (an electromagnetic field), there was born, in Einstein's words, "a new reality".

What had started as a method of understanding phenomena (epistemology) became progressively more a description of what is (ontology) so -

"The electromagnetic field is, for the modern physicist, as real as the chair on which he sits" (Einstein and Infield, 1938, pg151)

Ontological Reality and Relativistic Quantum Field Theory

Einstein (Einstein and Infield, 1936)) points out that science and physics is not just a collection of laws or facts – it is a creation of the human mind. The theories of physics are trying to form a picture of reality and link this to sense impressions. As Bohm has pointed out, our theories are not forms of knowledge of the world but forms of insight into the deeper nature of reality as a whole. (Bohm and Hiley 1993, page 322 and page 323) Both Bohm and Einstein note the role of imagination in this process as a nexus between that which is considered ontologically *real* and our experimental and mathematical methods which inform and interact with our consensus of what is indeed *real* by our senses. So processes such as physical observation, mathematics, theoretical conceptualisation, prediction and experimentation all interact to create a view of our world. While our sensory view may appear dominant, it is essentially only one view, and seemingly that of *appearances*. The physicist continually works to discover the *essence* of the appearances, and historically what happens is that what was once seen as essence later becomes a realized appearance.

Classical Reality

The Newtonian reality is one of separate objects and separate forces which act on these objects. This is the consensus reality of the western World in how we construct our state of consciousness and gives us a sense of separate identity and sense of a self. For 19th century physicists this presented a reality which was common sense experience and agreed with our intuitive understanding of the world (Einstein 1936, Bohm 1999, Lightman 2000).

The challenge to this view of reality arose in developing an understanding of processes which were essentially invisible yet the results of which clearly observable. The forces of gravity, magnetism, electricity and light all posed problems which then needed a new conceptualisation which Faraday and Maxwell introduced in the form of a field.

Field as Representation

The first stage of developing a field perspective of reality was to visualise and map as vectors the force that was acting in a field. At this point the field was used simply as a device, or method to help with conceptualisation. By drawing these lines of force such as gravity, physicists could note the direction of the force, but they could not use this as a way to explain gravity. In fact in a mechanical frame the speed of action of the force would need to be instantaneous as Newtons Laws only determined distance. So the attempt to make the field at this point *more* than a representation or model seemed fruitless (Einstein and Infield).

Field as Real

However while the representation model of the field was limited with gravity, it was the work with electricity, magnetism and then electromagnetism which began to prove the field as a reality. Maxwell's four equations defined the structure of the field. While Newton's laws defined the motion of the earth as affected by the force of a sun far away, Maxwell theory was about a field here and now as a whole and not two widely separated events. Therefore as Einstein and Infield relate, a new reality was created which described both electric and optical phenomena and the new concept of the field was the most important discovery in physics since Newton.

Field and Matter as Real

However various problems in the field, particularly the famous Michelson and Moreley experiment which set out to measure the effects of the field on the earth and instead found the speed of light to remain, unexpectedly, constant lead to developing the special and later general theories of relativity. These theories also developed a relationship between matter and energy showing mass is energy and energy has mass. Einstein and others had hoped this would lead to a Unified field theory, with matter as points of concentrated energy in the singular field. Having combined energy and matter in his equation he now needed to describe matter as a concentrated form of field.

As Einstein notes it became impossible to imagine a surface distinctly separating mass and field. This and the arrival of experiments that needed an acceptance of discontinuous quanta of energy and matter left Einstein with the unacceptable conclusion that he was left with two realities – matter and field.

"The theory of relativity stresses the importance of the field concept in physics. But we have not yet succeeded in formulating a pure field physics. For the present we must still assume the existence of both: field and matter." (Einstein and Infield pg 245)

It is the existence of these two realities, field and matter, as described by relativity and quantum physics together that leads to naming Relativistic Quantum Field theory (Bohm 1993, p351). Separately neither relativity theory nor quantum theory fully explains the phenomenon of light but together they do as relativistic quantum field theory.

Relativistic Quantum Physics - An Overview

The Laplacian world of classical physics is still available to our sensory awareness and is determined and measured and predictable using the laws of physics. Yet mathematics and experimental measurements display repeated evidence of a world which is invisible to our senses yet no less real, indeed more real than the sensory world. In fact the classical world is seen as a 'special case" of quantum reality where certain quantum effects are minimised or collapsed by our perception apparatus. Modern physics struggles between these two possibilities, yet has been forced to rely on theoretical description to explain quantum observations. In essence the physicists rely more and more on mathematics as a language to explain the results of measurements, knowing that such measurements are not the whole story. Before the 20th century, physics was primarily oriented to the direct sensory experience of reality and used mathematics to confirm the results. As quantum physics developed and the mathematics became more and more complicated and developed, a change happened in which the mathematics became the prime source of experiencing the universe and direct experience became less important. Bohm (1993) argues that this would work better as a movement between mathematics and experience so each supports and informs the other.

Quantum Reality

Quantum theory and quantum mechanics have developed to understand several experiments and observations which display the dual nature of reality. Taking light as a prime example, there are times when light behaves as if it were made up of particles or photons (such as the photoelectric effect) and times when it behaves as a wave phenomenon (such as bending light around an object). More interestingly there are times when light behaves as both a wave and a particle *depending on whether it is observed or not* (such as the double slit experiment). This has become known as the "wave-particle duality" This quantum view of reality traced four points, which challenge the relativistic and classical view of reality. The wave-particle duality just mentioned, the uncertainty of measurement leading to a probability based approach, the nature of the observer in determining reality, and non-locality. Bohr and Heisenberg were the main authors of the Uncertainty Principle which, unlike the previous views of reality, did not allow for individual measurements and predictions but only probability estimates of aggregates. Many people often confuse uncertainty with the role of the observer in determining reality. While the Uncertainty principle of Heisenberg tells us we effect the measurement by in essence "touching" that which is being measured and so "moving" it, a much more spectacular affect of the observer is found in the Double Slit Experiment where the nature of light or electrons changes between being a particle or a wave depending on whether it is observed.

The Challenge of Quantum Theory

From here the issues which are challenging our perceived Newtonian Reality as well as the special and general theories of relativity are:

- Wave Particle Duality;
- Non locality
- Reality and the inseparable relation of the observer and the observed;
- Uncertainty;

These four principle challenges to classical Newtonian reality by quantum theory can be described psychologically as Identity, Connection, Ontology and Control.

Quantum Identity and the Wave Particle Duality.

The nature of the world and tries to understand its basic composition can be traced to Democritus (Lightman, 2000) who postulated the basic building blocks of the universe are atoms. For many centuries two substances, energy and matter prevailed. Then with the arrival of the Special Theory of Relativity in the 20th century Einstein developed a synthesis, which integrated these two substances into one. This began a stage of physics in which a counter intuitive nature of reality was presented by physics. In short, the nature of reality in 20th century physics went against the common sense and our sensory experiences. In the famous Double Slit Experiment originated by Thomas Young, a dim light is passed through two slits unto a screen which produces a pattern. This pattern displays light acting as a wave phenomenon because the patterns produced show positive and negative interference in the forms of striated bands. If the light was acting as a particle they would instead produce two clearly defined bands of light.

However when non interfering glass monitors are attached to the slits they record each electron or photon as they passed through the slits. So the photon or electron is acting as a particle, as matter instead of field. When the photon or electron is observed it acts as a particle, yet when not observed the result is a wave phenomenon. This highlights not only that we need , as Einstein reports, two theories for light, matter and field, but the context of observation is also a key in deciding the identity of the light.

Quantum Connection and the phenomenon of Non Locality

Difficulties in the measurement and determination of outcome are already well known in general culture and the immortal uncertainty of this as defined by Heisenberg and Bohr are already a part of this undoing of classical physics. A greater challenge exists in the wave-particle duality of nature which is mediated by the observer. Each of these goes against common sense and intuition.

However the most emphatic description of a quantum experiment which challenges both classical physics and relativity is the 'EPR' experiment, named after Einstein, Polosky and Rosen. This famous experiment shows there is an effect between two seemingly separate halves of an atom which are spinning in opposite directions large distances apart. The results of this experiment are that one half is measured this causes a shift in the other immediately. Such a result displays "action at a distance" which shows a wave phenomenon however this effect happens at speed which is instantaneous and therefore violates the universal constant of light. It was this experiment that lead Einstein to decide that Quantum physics was incomplete. He stated that while this results existed, they "violated a small quiet voice"

Ontology and the Phenomenological role of the Observer

The place of the observer in creating the identity (wave or particle) was initially stressed by Bohr in what became known as the Copenhagen school. Working with Heisenberg they determined that either the momentum or the position of the photon could be determined but not both. This lead to Bohr insisting the whole phenomenon must be the object of study and not the reference to a particle or wave as this missed that complete picture of the phenomenon as whole.

Others such as Van Neuman developed the "many worlds" theory which stated that before a phenomenon was measured it existed in many different potentials, or worlds and the process of measurement created one of these worlds. Others still have preferred to keep the holism of the world and found many worlds untenable and instead have described this process in more phenomenological terms as the "many minds" theory.

Therefore each different possible measure of the phenomenon was a certain perspective of mind and so there are an infinite number of phenomenological realities possible at the quantum level.

The Mouse that Observed

Von Neuman postulated that observation induces a collapse of the wave function into single state (that is an observation where before there was a range of possibilities).

Einstein objected to this and said that he could not believe a mouse could bring about a drastic change in the universe simply by looking at it. Everett argued that it was not so much the system that was affected by an observation as it is the observer becomes correlated to the system. The mouse does not affect the universe – only the mouse is affected.

There also exists the possibility that each affects the other, and as the system is described by Bohr and Bohm as holistic and as the whole phenomenon, observation in this way still causes change. Awareness by and of itself, has an effect.

212

The Uncertainty of Quantum Control - Individuals and Crowds

Bohr felt the indivisibility of the wave and particle nature of a quantum of energy meant the entire phenomenon had to be regarded as a single unanalysable whole. It is this whole that makes up the entire quantum phenomenon. The uncertainty was the limits of certainty to which we could give to both the position and the momentum. As Einstein pointed out, the laws of quantum physics are statistical as they cannot adequately measure an individual system but a series of repeated measurements. There is not the slightest trace of a law to govern individual behavior but only that of large aggregations of atoms. This led him to state -

"Quantum physics deals only with aggregations, and its laws are for crowds and not for individuals"

(Einstein and Infield, p286)

213

A large crowd of people can be treated by a simple statistical law while individually their behavior is more subtle and complex. A particle moving under its own energy but being guided by information in the quantum field suggests elementary particles have a more complex and subtle inner structure A particle like a person has a rich and complex inner structure and can respond to information and influence form the field and direct its self motion accordingly.

If the field has already learnt something, the particle in the field will have its motion determined from quantum fields that have already experienced the phenomenon Qualitively new features of the quantum potential imply a novel quantum wholeness such the behavior of the particle may depend crucially on distant features of the environment. We cannot discuss the properties of a particular system apart from the context of the entire experimental arrangement with the aid of which these properties are observed.

The Most Fundamentally New Aspect of Quantum theory is the Whole is More Than the Sum of the Parts.

As we have seen in physics and biology, the nature of reality is a core issue and unfortunately there is not one clear theoretical definition. At present there is matter and field. There exists a tension between relativity and quantum physics, particularly around the phenomenon of non-locality, and this has been instrumental in physicists to developing theories which accommodate both, such as Bohm's holomovement and the Implicate Order.

In a description closely approximating that of Perls, Hefferline and Goodman, Bohm and others define classical reality as rising

215

out of the ground of the quantum field. Such a process of collapsing a wave phenomenon mathematically leads to describing the classical physical world as a special limited case of quantum reality and the concept of independent existence is, as in Perls, Hefferline and Goodman, an illusion. Yet as Bohm points out the illusion rests in seeing the classical world as the whole. Once it is seen to be merely a facet it is no longer an illusion.

The Mathematics of Consciousness

Quantum mechanics has shifted from world where the physicist could justifiably stand outside of that which was being measured, to a world where the measurement and act of measuring decides the nature of that which is being measured. So the observer has become part of the mathematical equation and this has lead to mathematics of awareness where the awareness of one observer (person or computer) is defined as an equation.

These mathematical equations are more sophisticated examples of the quasi mathematical modeling done by Lewin. He was still describing a much wider phenomenon such as behavior, yet the first steps towards this are now in the application of mathematics by physicists to define and include awareness as part of quantum theory. Such steps have then lead to the inclusion and description of consciousness as a quantum phenomenon. Bohm in particular presents consciousness as a process unfolding and enfolding between the classical world and the quantum world - a bridge between both which is in part a particle or matter phenomenon and in part a quantum field effect. This bridging process of consciousness in quantum physics is important as we look to the potential applications of relativistic quantum field theory to Gestalt therapy. Consciousness, awareness and observation are now at the heart of quantum physics. In trying to decide at what point quantum reality "collapses" into classical Newtonian reality of our senses, a key process, as we have seen, is that of observation and awareness.

In essence, the quantum world is subtle and the ultimate ground of existence out of which the classical world arises and becomes manifest and *relatively* autonomous. The role of awareness then plays an important role in joining these two rather contradictory views of reality - matter and field. As Bohm states -

"From this it follows that we are directly aware of the particle aspect of the universe through our senses and that the more subtle wave function aspect is inferred by thought about our sensory

experiences in the domain that is manifest to the senses."

(Bohm 1999 p314)

Therefore the classical world of matter that our senses perceive is constantly made figural by our awareness and consciousness from of the more subtle ground of the field nature of reality. The figure/ground process is not only in operation with sensory data of the visible world, but with the subtle experience of the invisible world of the field.

As Bohm puts it -

"The Quantum world observes itself and the quantum measurement is a manifesting process" (ibid pg 179)

This important role of consciousness in linking matter and field, manifest and subtle realty, highlights crucial functions of the therapist. As already predicted by gestalt therapists, awareness by and of itself has an affect on reality. Our ability to be aware of bridging these two realities of field and matter means that we are instruments of the field.

Active Information and quantum fields

In the Double Slit Experiment as previously described, a group of particles with the same quantum field will pass through the double slit system to then be detected eventually on a screen. These particles are usually photons or electrons. Each individual result is determined by the first condition of the particle and each particle must pass through one slit or the other. The motion of the particle as it passes through a slit is determined by information in the quantum field as a whole, so there exists what is called "active information" in the quantum field. As the particle reaches certain points in front of the slits, it is "in-formed" to accelerate or decelerate accordingly, sometimes violently (Bohm p 37). So the information in the quantum field that accompanies a particle which has already passed through either slit is available to the particles as they pass through. This is a field phenomenon which in essence also explains non-locality. These qualitatively new features of the quantum potential imply novel quantum wholeness such the behavior of the particle may depend crucially on distant features of the environment. Further there exists information in the field as a whole which is accessible to the individual particles and influences them.

The Effect is in the Form of the Field not the Intensity

An effect of quantum fields well worth considering in relationship to psychotherapy is a phenomenon in which the affect of a field is not determined by its intensity but only by its form. This is so different in the classical reality where the affect, or ability to do work, is in direct relation to the available force, so for example to move a ship needs a great amount of energy. On the contrary in the quantum field, a very weak field can produce a full quantum affect as this is related solely to the form and not the intensity of the field.

In many ways this is more like the effect of a radio signal telling a ship where to go, where the radio wave is not directly pushing or pulling the ship that it guides. The action of Quantum Potential depends only on form not magnitude and so effect may be dominant even when intensity is small. This implies strong non-local connection of distant particles and strong dependence on its general environmental context.

Passive and Active Information

Bohm talks of passive information which also plays a role in influencing the field and the behavior of the particle. He considers the literal meaning of information as to being to in-form, which is actively to put form into something or imbue it with form. (Bohm 1993, p.35) He considers how processes such as radio waves are *potentially* active everywhere and become active when it can give form to electrical energy. Other structures which exist as principally passive information are computer chips which hold so much information and even DNA.

Wholeness and Independent existence

Quantum field theory, relativistic quantum field theory and the holographic field theory of Bohm present a view of reality and the self closely akin to that of Gestalt therapy.

223

From the beginnings of quantum physics, Bohr felt the results of the experiments and his work and that of Heisenberg, needed a new approach in which the whole phenomenon, including the observation and observing apparatus was to be regarded as a single and unanalysable whole (ibid p15).

Quantum theory has not been united with the special or general theories of relativity in a generally agreed on and this is mainly due to several points of inconsistency, particularly non-locality (Einstein and Infield, Lightman, Bohm and Hiley p351). Yet as Bohm points out, rather than consider the differences between these theories, a clue to their convergence maybe found in their commonality.

The key element their share in common is unbroken wholeness. (Bohm p352).

Specifically individual identity as described by Bohm's idea of implicate order and the holomovement, is a clear parallel to the process of figure/ground and the gestalt therapy theory of the self.

He notes the idea of a permanent entity with a given identity (self) is at best an approximation (illusion) whether this be a particle or anything else (ibid p357).

Interestingly in Bohm as in Perls, Hefferline and Goodman, it is contact which denotes identity yet this identity is one in which the basic elements are constantly forming and dissolving in succession.

Bibliography.

Bohm, D & Hiley, B.J. (1993). The Undivided Universe. Routledge, London.

Bohr, N. (1961) Atomic Physics and Human Knowledge, Science Editions, New York.

Bowman, C. (2005). The History and Development of Gestalt Therapy in Woldt, A. and Toman, S.(2005) Gestalt Therapy: History, Theory, Practice. SAGE Publications, Thousand Oaks.

Buber, M., (1958) I-Thou, Scribner Books, New York

Capra, F. (1982) The Tao of Physics, Flamingo, London.

Crocker, S. (1999) A Well Lived Life: Essays in Gestalt Therapy. GIC Press Cleveland

Einstein, A & Infield, L. (1938) The Evolution of Physics. Simon and Schuster, New York

Ellis, W. ed.,(1938 reprinted 1997). A Source Book of Gestalt Psychology. The Gestalt Journal Press, New York

Gibran, K. (1924). *The Prophet*. NY: Alfred A. Knopf, Inc.

Hycner, R. (1995). The Healing Relationship in Gestalt Therapy: A Dialogic – Self-Psychology Approach.

Fagan, J and Shepherd, I.L. The Tasks of the Therapist in Fagan, J. and Shepherd, I.L. (1970) Gestalt Therapy Now, Science and Behavior Books, Palo Alto.

Francis, T.(2005). Working with the Field. British Gestalt Journal,14,1, pp 26-33.

Hamlyn, D.W. (1987) The Penguin History of Western Philosophy. Penguin Books, London.

James, W. (1902) The Varieties of Religious Experience, 1977 Fontana Paperback, Glasgow.

Kempler. W., (1974) Principles of Gestalt Family Therapy, Kempler Institute, California.

Kepner, J. (1995) Healing Tasks: Psychotherapy with Adult Survivors of Childhood Abuse. Jossey-Bass and Gestalt Institute of Cleveland, San Francisco.

Latner, J. (1983) This is the speed of light: Field and systems theory in Gestalt therapy. The Gestalt Journal 6,2 (Fall 1983), 71-90

Lee, R.(Ed) (2004) The Values of Connection: A Relational Approach to Ethics. Gestalt

Institute Cleveland Press, Cleveland.

Lee, R., (2008) The Secret Language of Intimacy, Routledge Press/Gestalt Press, USA.

Le Shan, (1974) The Medium, the Mystic and the Physicist. Ballantine Books, New York

Lewin, K. (1936) Principles of Topological Psychology. McGraw-Hill, New York

Lewin, K.(1951) Field Theory in Social Science. University of Chicago Press, Chicago.

Lightman, A (2000). Great Ideas in Physics. McGraw-Hill, New York

Mackewen, J.(1997). Developing Gestalt Counselling, Sage Publications, London.

McNamara, W., (1979). "Mystical Passion - The Art of Christian Loving" San Francisco: Harper & Row, pages 57-58

McTaggart, L. (2003) The Field. Harper Collins, London.

Mitchell, S. (translator) (2000) The Bhagavad Bhagavad Gita. Three Rivers Press, New York.

Nicoll, M (1976) Living Time and the Integration of Life. Watkins, London.

Ornstein, R. (1972) The Psychology of Consciousness, Penguin, New York

O'Neill, B., Post Relativistic Quantum Field Theory and Gestalt Therapy, *Gestalt Review*, Vol 12, no 1, 2008, pps 7-23.

O'Neill, B., & O'Neill, J. The Use of Group in Training, in Feder, R., Beyond the Hot

Seat: Group Approaches in Gestalt Therapy, Gestalt Institute Press, USA, 2008

O'Neill, B., & O'Neill, J. (2008) Field Theory and Couples Therapy, in Lee, R., The Secret Language of Intimacy, Routledge Press/Gestalt Press, USA,

O'Neill, B., & Gaffney, S. (2008) The Application of a Field Perspective Methodology, in Brownell, P., Handbook for Theory, Research and Practice in Gestalt Therapy, Cambridge Scholars Publishing, Cambridge.

O'Neill, B. (2012) Gestalt Family Therapy in Levine Bar-Yoseph, T., (ed) New Approaches to Gestalt Therapy, Routledge, London.

Parlett, M.(1993). Towards a More Lewian Gestalt Therapy, British Gestalt Journal 2,2 p. 115-121

Parlett, M.(1997). The Unified Field in Practice. Gestalt Review, 1,1 p.16-33

Parlett, M. (2005) Contemporary Gestalt Therapy: Field Theory in Woldt, A. & Toman, S. Gestalt Therapy: History, Theory and Practice. Sage Publications, Thousand Oaks.

Perls, F., Hefferline, R., and Goodman, P. (1951) Gestalt Therapy: Excitement and Growth in the Human Personality. Souvenir Press edition (1984) London.

Philippson. P. (2001) Self in Relation. Gestalt Journal Press, New York.

Polster, E. & Polster, M. (1973) Gestalt therapy integrated: Contours of theory and practice. Brunner-Mazel, New York.

Polster, E & Polster, M. (1999) From the

Radical Center: The Heart of Gestalt Therapy. GIC Press, Cleveland.

Resnick, R. (1995). Gestalt therapy: Principles, prisms and perspectives. British Gestalt Journal,4(1),3-13.

Robine, J.(2001) From Field to Situation in Robine, J (Ed) Contact and Relationship in a Field Perspective. L'experimerie Bordeaux.

Sheldrake, R.(2003) The Sense of Being Stared At and other aspects of the Extended Mind. Random House, London.

Shepard, M (1976) Fritz. Bantam, New York

Smuts, J. (1926) edited by Holst, S. (1999) Holism and Evolution: The Original Source of the Holistic Approach to Life. Sierra Sunrise Books.

Staemmler, F.M. (2006). A Babylonian

Confusion? – The Term Field. The British Gestalt Journal, 15:2 : 64-83

Swedenborg, E. (1768, 1992) Conjugial Love, Swedenborg Foundation, New York
Swedenborg, E. (1758, edition 2009) Heaven and Its Wonders and Hell, Swedenborg Foundation, New York pg 31-32

Talbot, M.(1991) The Holographic Universe. Harper Collins, London.

Tart, C. (1975) States of Consciousness. E P Dutton and Co, New York.

Van Dusen, W. (1975) Invoking the Actual, in Stevens, J.O., gestalt is, Real People Press, Moab.

Wheeler, G (1991) Gestalt Reconsidered: A New Approach to Contact and Resistance. GIC Press, Cleveland.

Wheeler, G. (2000). *Beyond Individualism: Towards a New Understanding of Self, Relationship and Experience*. Hillsdale, NJ: Gestalt Institute of Cleveland Press.

Van Dusen, W. (2001). *The Design of Existence*. Chrysalis Books, West Chester,

Wertheimer, M. Gestalt Theory. (1925) in Ellis, W. ed.,(1938 reprinted 1997). A Source Book of Gestalt Psychology.The Gestalt Journal Press, New York

Wilber, K. (ed) (1985) The Holographic Paradigm and Other Paradoxes. Shambhala, Boston & London.

Yontef, G. (1993) Awareness, Dialogue and Process: Essays of Gestalt Therapy. The Gestalt Journal Press, New York,

Zinker, J. (1994) In search of good form: Gestalt therapy with couples and families.

Jossey- Bass, San Francisco.